"THE STRANGER WITHIN THEE"

Stephen D. Cox

"The Stranger Within Thee"

CONCEPTS OF THE SELF
IN LATE-EIGHTEENTH-CENTURY
LITERATURE

UNIVERSITY OF PITTSBURGH PRESS

Published by the University of Pittsburgh Press, Pittsburgh, Pa. 15260
Copyright © 1980, University of Pittsburgh Press
All rights reserved
Feffer and Simons, Inc., London
Manufactured in the United States of America

Library of Congress Cataloging in Publication Data

Cox, Stephen D 1948–
  "The stranger within thee."

  Includes bibliographical references and index.
    1. English literature – 18th century – History and
criticism. 2. Self in literature. 3. Psychology
and literature. I. Title.
PR449.S45C6   820'.9353   80-5252
ISBN 0-8229-3424-8

To my parents, Donald and Dorothy Cox

Contents

Acknowledgments

It is a pleasure to express my gratitude for the help I have received from many sources. G. S. Rousseau advised me on the direction of my research and gave incisive criticism to work in progress. Walter H. Evert, Maximillian Novak, Paul Sheats, Ross Shideler, and Donald S. Taylor read my manuscript and offered me counsel and encouragement. A Chancellor's Fellowship from the University of California, Los Angeles, supported me during the early stages of planning and writing. The William Andrews Clark Memorial Library and the Henry E. Huntington Library provided me with excellent facilities for study. Louise Craft, my editor, and Beth Luey, my copy editor, guided my work calmly and efficiently through the press. My students, Michael Schein and Richard Krecker, helped me in preparing the typescript and correcting proofs; no one could ask for more intelligent assistance or a more patient audience.

"THE STRANGER WITHIN THEE"

CHAPTER ONE

The Self as Stranger

In 1759, in his *Conjectures on Original Composition*, Edward Young gave this counsel to beginning authors: "*Know thyself*. . . . learn the depth, extent, biass, and full fort of thy mind; contract full intimacy with the Stranger within thee."[1] Advice as old as the Delphic oracle — but it took on new meaning for many writers of the later eighteenth century. In Young's *Conjectures*, self-knowledge means more than examining one's powers and motives honestly; it also means coming to know the creative self as something unique and "original." But the problem of discovering one's "original genius" is only one aspect of a more general problem of self-knowledge that assumes crucial importance in much of the period's literature: the whole question of defining what is distinctive, and distinctively valuable, about the individual self.

This book is a study of eighteenth-century efforts to conceptualize what Young called the "naked self"[2] — efforts that ordinarily involved an attempt to "contract full intimacy" with what is most basic to the self: its processes of "feeling" and perception, its powers of "sensibility." But the very concept of sensibility often posed great difficulties for authors who endeavored to express the workings of the individual mind. My study of the literature of sensibility suggests the ironic fact that the more ardently the self is pursued, the more elusive that "stranger" may become.

Although I am concerned primarily with the literature of the later eighteenth century, it is obvious that problems of the self have arisen, in some form, in the cultural life of every civilization. Even ancient Buddhism, with its emphasis on selflessness, had its debates about the self; during the Personalist controversy, a numerous sect maintained that a continuous self must exist or there would be nothing capable of knowledge, while the orthodox argued that "in fact this so-called 'personality' is nothing but a series of consecutive impersonal events, all of them linked to suffering."[3] Problems of the self have always been a part — usually a prominent part — of Western philosophy and literature, and it is far from simple to determine which of them may be considered in some way distinctive of any particular literary "period."

In any age, these problems may assume a variety of different forms. It would be easy to compile a long list of them: What is the self? Is it merely an obstacle to spiritual growth, or is it something to be valued for its own sake? Is it the same in nature and in dignity as the soul, or is it merely a reflection of sense experience and social conditioning? Does each person possess an essential and consistent identity, or may the self be expected to change under the influence of its environment and, perhaps, multiply into various and competing selves? In what ways does the self resist or assimilate its experience? Where lie its sources of creativity? The list might be extended indefinitely. All of these questions are, in one way or another, related; and each of them may easily evoke all the rest. It is difficult to know where to begin in considering them. If one adds the strictly personal problems that dispose a particular author to take an interest in examining the self, the difficulty begins to seem insuperable.

And yet the very fact that all of these problems appear to be related may help one to find order among them. It is possible that most questions of this nature that exert any considerable influence on life or art are ultimately related to two central issues: first, the problem of personal identity (Who am I?) and second, the problem of personal significance (What is the value or importance of this "I"?). The first arises when one attempts to define the self; it may include the problem of deciding what the concept of identity or individuality means in the abstract, but it more often reduces to the question of defining what attitudes or characteristics make up a person's "true self" or "fundamental nature." The problem of personal significance arises when one attempts to find standards by which to evaluate the self or asks questions about its dignity or creative potential. In literary studies, a consideration of both these problems of the self is important: what an author assumes about the essential nature of the self is of course very likely to influence his works; but what he believes, or has been taught to believe, about the qualities that give significance to self and self-expression is no less likely to have its effect. Furthermore, these two problems are almost inseparable: the impulse to define the nature of the self normally originates in a desire to establish its significance, but one's idea of the self's value is often determined by the very means one uses to define the self.

These, then, are the two major problems whose effects on the literature of sensibility will principally concern us. The fact that these issues have arisen so frequently in life and in literature may, perhaps, impart something of general interest to a study of their effect on one particular period. At any time, a difficulty in solving these problems may cause the self to appear as a "stranger." Yet one must recognize the fact that the specific forms these two problems assume in particular periods may vary in response to the material circumstances and philosophical interests of each age. Although artists of different centuries may be aware of similar problems, they may perceive and respond to them differently. Twentieth-century literature, as everyone knows, has been strongly affected by an awareness of the individual's lack of significance in modern society; in order to find some means of dramatizing the individual self and its anxieties, contemporary writers have exploited the resources made available to them by such disparate movements as existential psychology, Freudian analysis, and hastily revised forms of mysticism. In the Renaissance, to cite an extremely contrasting example, artists concerned with the problem of personal significance could turn more easily to the idea of a stable moral and social order to find a way of defining the value of the self.

Such examples are simple and obvious, but they must not be allowed to mislead us. Literary "periods" cannot easily be defined, and no two authors in any given "period" respond in precisely the same way to any general problem. With this kept firmly in mind, however, we may be able to learn something about a number of different authors by viewing them from a common perspective. Certain ideas, certain ways of approaching personal or literary problems, may for a time become so prominent and authoritative that they elicit a common interest, though not necessarily a common response, from authors who otherwise differ widely from one another.

This is true, I believe, of certain related attitudes toward self and sensibility that appear with great frequency and emphasis in the literature of the later eighteenth century — attitudes that were strongly influenced, directly or indirectly, by the psychology of Locke and his successors. A study of these attitudes may provide one way of gaining perspective on the great variety of works produced in that age. One must, however, be especially wary in discussing a literary period about which it is notoriously difficult to make convincing generalizations. One may easily recognize the influence of empirical psychology in countless poems, novels, and aesthetic treatises of the later eighteenth century,[4] but one should also consider the fact that the concepts of self that developed in association with empirical psychology affected literature in a number of different ways, ways that were often fundamentally inconsistent with one another.

The tendency of empirical psychology is to regard the self principally as a creation of its perceptions, and one would expect literature affected by this attitude to be especially concerned with the self as a reflection of its education and experience. We need not look far in eighteenth-century literature to find a belief in society's ability to mold individual values, coupled with a belief in the possession of the "social passions" as an indication of personal significance. But there is also sufficient evidence of another, inherently contradictory belief — two beliefs, really, that reach their fullest expression in the literature of the early nineteenth century: a conviction that the individual self and its original "feelings" are of the utmost value, and an analogous conviction that spontaneous self-expression is of the highest aesthetic significance. On the one hand, psychological, moral, and literary theory exalted the self's outer-directed social "sympathy"; on the other hand, it insisted on the importance of the inner qualities that make the self an autonomous being, qualities such as "original genius" or the "moral sense." Many of the concepts with which late-eighteenth-century writers were most concerned were marked by the influence of such contradictory views of the self. "Sensibility" was regarded both as an expression of individual character and as a beneficial agent of "self-annihilation"; the "sublime," that great inspiration of eighteenth-century art, was considered simultaneously to dramatize and "absorb" the self; and even "genius" was depicted as both creative independence and emotional "ductility" and susceptibility.

Nothing is more common in eighteenth-century literature and philosophy than the search for the "true self," a self that is often rather conveniently regarded both as an individual's "real" identity and as the principle from which he can derive the greatest moral significance. Yet this essential self proves very difficult to discover and express. The "true self" frequently appears as a mysterious presence, portentous yet indistinct, and the hesitancy of its manifestations can be attributed, in large part, to the assumption that the self can best be understood as the embodiment of its "feelings" — its perceptions and emotional responses. This method of approaching the self may produce results very different from those of methods more often favored in other ages: defining the self by its established social roles, for example, or analyzing the position of "man" in the structure of the universe, the method that the *nosce teipsum* treatises of the English Renaissance often employed.[5] The eighteenth century's emphasis on "sensibility" is an emphasis on the way in which the individual self apprehends the world. From this standpoint, it may seem, in the words of Blake's paraphrase of Locke's theory, that man "is only a natural organ subject to Sense"[6] and that the self changes as its experience changes. When one recognizes, in addition, that individual impulses and habits of perception make "sensibility" a medium by means of which experience is altered as well as absorbed, then one may begin to question whether all principles of identity or significance may not be purely subjective illusions.

In his study of eighteenth-century aesthetics, Ernest Lee Tuveson has observed that empirical psychology created the problem of "reconstructing on new foundations the dignity of the soul" — a dignity that came increasingly to be based, in the works of the moralists and aestheticians whom Tuveson considers, on subjective and imaginative experience.[7] This, of course, is the movement that culminates in Romantic theories of the creative self. One of the primary interests of eighteenth-century philosophers and artists, however, was to escape from the threat that subjectivity posed to the dignity of the self. They sought some inherent shape in the fluctuating medium of sensibility, some stable principle on which personal significance could be based; and many believed that they could find it in such "inherent capacities" as the moral sense and, especially, the controlling impulse to social "sympathy."

"Self-approving joy," in the literature of sensibility, is most often a delight in one's sympathetic, ostensibly selfless, impulses; and there are good reasons, even apart from those that could easily be drawn from social history, why a literature that was so generally based upon "feeling" and a nascent individualism should so rarely have developed in the direction of explicit individualism and hedonism, but should have turned so frequently instead to the milder joys of social sympathy. One explanation is suggested by A. D. Nuttall's analysis of the problem of solipsism in empirical psychology and in the literature of the past two centuries.[8] Renaissance poets, he observes, often describe the self as viewing the world through the clear windows of the senses, but this imagery is too simple and straightforward to represent post-Lockean attitudes toward the process of perception. Empirical philosophers suggested that the mind has only indirect knowledge of what lies outside itself; its sense "impressions" are its only guides, and there is no proof that they acquaint it with reality. In the eighteenth century and after, such thinking sometimes led to a fear of solipsism and to a corresponding need for emotional reassurance that the self is not an isolated being. Of course, as Nuttall himself remarks, solipsism is a matter of temperament as well as philosophy. At no time would we expect it to be a general affliction; not every poet is a young Wordsworth, grasping at walls to convince himself that the outside world is real. We do, however, see a strong awareness, in eighteenth-century literature and philosophy, of the ways in which the self may be isolated by its subjective sensibility. From such an awareness, and not merely from a sentimental humanism, the eighteenth century's enthusiasm about the power of sympathy derived much of its inspiration. Sympathy is an impulse or, more properly, a form of sensibility that connects the inner with the outer world. But for this very reason, when it is regarded as something that gives shape and significance to the individual self, distinctions between the self conditioned by society and the self defined by inner principle become difficult to maintain: the "true self" wavers on the margin of two worlds.

I have attempted to suggest some of the important questions that arise concerning the concept of self as it appears in the literature of the later eighteenth century. In the following chapters I will explore each of these questions more fully. It may be useful to state at the outset that although modern schools of psychology — behaviorism, Freudianism, the several forms of "humanist" or "existentialist" thought — have much to say about problems of conceptualizing the self, my primary concern is with psychological problems as they were apprehended by eighteenth-century writers. I have therefore preferred to approach eighteenth-century texts directly, rather than through the medium of any particular modern theory, and to discipline my discussion to avoid imposing strictly modern categories of thought upon the eighteenth century. Furthermore, in deciding to focus on certain eighteenth-century attitudes toward the problems of personal identity and significance, I necessarily recognize that I have decided not to focus on a number of other issues, including the political and economic "individualism" of the middle class, the evolution of various concepts of nature and order, and the traditional conflict, which persisted in the works of many writers of the later eighteenth century, between reason and the "passions." All of these subjects are, of course, related to the question of the self; all of them deserve, and have received, extensive study. But I have chosen to investigate problems in literature and psychological theory that are, I believe, important in their own right; and I hope that what I have to say on this subject will be seen in its proper relation to other issues in eighteenth-century thought.

I have not attempted to review every literary work of the later eighteenth century that presents some concept of the self—an impossible task, and one that might produce more complexity than enlightenment even if it were fulfilled. I have chosen, instead, to analyze in some depth the problems of the self that appear in the works of Samuel Richardson, Thomas Gray, Thomas Chatterton, William Cowper, and William Blake. One of my reasons for selecting these authors is, obviously enough, the fact that their works appear to me to have enduring value. Another reason is the desire to include authors of widely different views and interests so that I can examine a variety of responses to the basic problems of identity and significance. A consideration of Blake is especially useful in a study of this kind; his psychological theory supplies a commentary on his predecessors' concepts of the self and provides an opportunity to determine the extent to which a radical Romanticism could free itself from the problems that arose in the literature of sensibility. Choice of authors is perhaps the most onerous task involved in preparing a study of an era as rich in discussions of the self as the later eighteenth century; my failure to discuss an author does not imply that I think his views uninteresting or unimportant. At least one of my omissions, however, ought to be particularly accounted for—my decision not to provide a detailed examination of the works of Samuel Johnson. Probably no one in the later eighteenth century was so profound a student of himself and others, but the same common sense that allowed Johnson to refute Berkeley by kicking a stone generally kept him from involving his works in the peculiarly complicated problems of identity and significance that are characteristic of the literature of sensibility.

But no matter whose works are chosen for study, a series of essays on a necessarily short list of authors probably cannot fairly indicate the scope of eighteenth-century speculation on the self. It might not succeed even in illuminating the background of those authors' own ideas. Before discussing the five authors I have selected, I will try to place their views in context by examining some of the more significant concepts of self developed in eighteenth-century psychological theory. Each of these writers was influenced, of course, not just by contemporary ideas about the self, but also by his own artistic motives and psychological needs. One would expect problems of the self to be more interesting to people who already felt some deep insecurity about their own position in the world, and this is emphatically true of some of the writers I will examine. It was not books of philosophy that started Gray and Cowper worrying about the self; it was, more likely, unresolved sexual conflicts in the one and a manic-depressive condition in the other. A strictly biographical approach might seem natural to use in analyzing such authors, but it might obscure the fact that an artist's work is not entirely the product of his personal needs or frustrations; it also develops in response to the common assumptions of his time. He may reject or affirm those ideas, or modify them to fit his personal needs, but in any case they help to establish his categories of thought. Jean A. Perkins remarks, in her study of the self as it was viewed in the French Enlightenment, that people's notions and expectations of themselves tend to conform to their philosophical notions of the self, and the same might be said of authors' notions of their characters' "selves."[9] One must remind oneself that one should not be concerned so much with restating well-known biographical information as with investigating what ideas might have been available to authors struggling to solve the problems of the self of which they were aware. In addition, an understanding of the many intellectual problems involved in defining the self's nature and significance may sharpen one's perception of the difficulties encountered by authors who attempted to create a satisfactory concept of the self — even when it is apparent that these authors were by no means preoccupied with purely philosophical problems.

It is for these reasons, then, that I have provided an analysis of self and sensibility in eighteenth-century psychological theory. The views of prominent philosophers must of course be considered, not just on the more technical problems of identity but also on the question, which is more directly relevant to literature, of what constitutes a "true" and morally significant self. In addition, it is necessary to examine the concepts of self that gained influence through the works of literary critics and theorists. Theories of the creative self are perhaps as helpful as the works of philosophers and moralists in understanding eighteenth-century and Romantic attitudes toward personal identity and significance. As I will suggest, for instance, Chatterton's method of dramatizing the self shows an attempt to assimilate a variety of popular notions regarding not only the moral value of sensibility but also the nature of original genius, and Blake's psychological theory can hardly be understood without considering his attitude toward those two most common topics of late-eighteenth-century literary discourse.

Sydney Shoemaker, a modern philosopher interested in the problem of personal identity, has observed that "most of us have the feeling . . . that we do not really understand the nature of a thing unless we can imagine or picture it," and that a difficulty in picturing the self — particularly as something distinct from a body — can make "persons seem a mysterious sort of objects."[10] The problem is complicated by the fact that to be considered meaningful, a "picture," "image," or "model" of the self must generally be of the kind that makes it possible to assert the self's significance. This is especially necessary if a conception of the self is to be useful for literary purposes; as a recent book by Patricia Meyer Spacks suggests, the act of writing about the self almost requires one to find a way of imagining a significant self.[11] The common eighteenth-century assumption that the self is a creature of perceptions, feelings, and sensibility made it difficult indeed to find a clear image of the self; but, as I will show, that assumption did make it easy for writers of the eighteenth century not only to develop anxieties about the self, but also to surround it with an aura of mystery and power.

CHAPTER TWO

Eighteenth-Century
Philosophies of Self

It is well to begin the discussion of eighteenth-century concepts of self with the book to which eighteenth-century theories of psychology are most frequently indebted, John Locke's *Essay Concerning Human Understanding* (1690). This work, more than any other, established the authority of empirical psychology and suggested the methods by which the philosophy of the period approached the problems of personal identity and significance. And it was primarily this work that placed the whole question of perception, and of the mind's sensibility to what it perceives, at the heart of eighteenth-century attempts to determine the nature of the self.

It may be useful to state at once some of the more obvious features of Locke's philosophy, features that were thoroughly familiar to educated people of the eighteenth century. Locke argues that *"Self* is that conscious thinking thing . . . which is sensible, or conscious of Pleasure and Pain, capable of Happiness or Misery"; personal identity continues the same "as far as . . . consciousness can be extended backwards to any past Action or Thought."[1] None of the self's ideas are innate; they are, instead, the products of sense experience. The self forms many of its ideas by reflecting on its own mental operations, but these operations are ultimately dependent on its perceptions of the outside world, perceptions produced by matter in ways that are "incomprehensible to us."[2] The "primary qualities" that we perceive in external objects — bulk, figure, number, motion — actually exist in those objects, but the "secondary qualities" — sounds, colors, smells, tastes — are, as we know them, formed in the process of perception.[3] Not only is the self dependent on its individual experience for all its knowledge of the world — and one would think that such experience must naturally be rather subjective — but also, at least to some degree, the act of perception is really an act of creation.

The Lockean idea of creative perception is very limited, but it provided the eighteenth century with one way of exalting the self and its sensibility. In the *Spectator* (1712), Addison exploits the doctrine of secondary qualities to describe the perceiving self as the agent of a continual act of magic: if our senses did not create the "imaginary Glories" of light and color, the external world would remain but "a rough unsightly Sketch of Nature."[4] In his *Night Thoughts* (1742–45), Edward Young employs a similar argument to assert that the true "riches" of the self are inherent in its sensibility:

> Our *senses*, as our *reason*, are divine.
> But for the magic organ's pow'rful charm,
> Earth were a rude, uncolour'd chaos, still.
>
> . . . .
>
> Like *Milton's Eve*, when gazing on the lake,
> Man makes the matchless image, man admires.

In the phrase Wordsworth echoes in *Tintern Abbey*, Young proclaims that the senses "half create the wond'rous world they see." Locke's concept of perception has changed into something that Locke himself might have had difficulty recognizing, but the metamorphosis enables Young to find a place in the established order of creation for an ideal of psychological autonomy:

> Say then, Shall man, his thoughts all sent abroad,
> Superior wonders in himself forgot,
> His admiration waste on objects round,
> When Heav'n makes him the soul of all he sees?[5]

Unfortunately, however, for those who felt as Young did, it is also possible to use Locke's theory of the mind to emphasize the self's conditioning by the outside world. Such an emphasis is particularly prominent in the associationist psychology that was systematized by David Hartley in his *Observations on Man* (1749). Hartley describes the mind as a structure of associated ideas derived from its perceptions of the outside world; the way in which the self has been conditioned by its experience establishes individual character. The basic theory of associationism implies nothing very favorable about the inherent significance of the self; to solve that problem, Hartley places associationism at the service of his own moral and religious beliefs and views the conditioning of the self by its experience as a potential growth in reason, moral awareness, and social conscience.

On the basis of Locke's ideas, one may choose to regard the self as either creative or conditioned, but in each case, one may be led to doubt the self's ability to gain objective knowledge from its experience. This problem is only latent in Young's praise of man's ability to convert the natural world into an image of himself. But the peculiar quality of Locke's empiricism — indeed, of much of the empiricist psychology that was based on Locke — is that, although it seemingly reduces the self to complete dependence on its perceptions of the external world, it also invites questions about the self's ability to know that world.

These questions are explicit in the philosophy of Berkeley and Hume. In *The Principles of Human Knowledge* (1710), Berkeley asks why primary qualities, any more than secondary qualities, should inhere in matter. He concludes, of course, that they do not: the external world does not exist as matter but only as mental perceptions that God infuses into the self. Except for its dependence on the Deity, the self, in Berkeley's theory, may be regarded as solipsistic.

Empiricism led Berkeley to theological idealism, but it was to lead David Hume to an urbane scepticism and agnosticism. In the *Treatise of Human Nature* (1739–40), he adopts the Lockean principle that "nothing is ever really present with the mind but its perceptions or impressions and ideas, and that external objects become known to us only by those perceptions they occasion."[6] The problem, however, is deciding what we can really know from our perceptions. We cannot directly perceive a distinction between the inner world of the self and the outer world of material objects: "'Tis absurd . . . to imagine the senses can ever distinguish betwixt ourselves and external objects" (*Treatise*, p. 190). It is natural and necessary that we should believe in an external world that exists independently of our perceptions, but our belief is really the result of an act of "imagination" that unites a number of distinct impressions of objects into an appearance of continued reality (*Treatise*, pp. 187–218). In addition, Hume finds no experiential evidence for believing that the self is anything but its perceptions:

For my part, when I enter most intimately into what I call *myself*, I always stumble on some particular perception or other, of heat or cold, light or shade, love or hatred, pain or pleasure. I never can catch *myself* at any time without a perception, and never can observe any thing but the perception. . . . If any one upon serious and unprejudic'd reflexion, thinks he has a different notion of *himself*, I must confess I can reason no longer with him. . . . He may, perhaps, perceive something simple and continu'd, which he calls *himself*; tho' I am certain there is no such principle in me.

But setting aside some metaphysicians of this kind, I may venture to affirm of the rest of mankind, that they are nothing but a bundle or collection of different perceptions, which succeed each other with an inconceivable rapidity, and are in a perpetual flux and movement. (*Treatise*, p. 252)

In dealing with the question of self and perception, Berkeley and Hume found that they must resort, in Hume's phrase, "to the most profound metaphysics" (*Treatise*, p. 189). Hume specifically denied an intention of directing his theories to a popular audience (*Treatise*, p. 272); and, despite the assertion of one eighteenth-century journal that metaphysical scepticism had nearly attained an "empire universally absolute over the sentiments of the fashionable part of mankind," it is doubtful that either Berkeley or Hume ever had a direct and decisive influence on a large number of readers.[7] Their greatest influence was probably exerted indirectly, through other philosophers' attempted refutations of their ideas. The members of the "Common Sense" school were particularly active in attempting to devise a theory of the perceiving self in opposition to the theories of Berkeley and Hume, and, as I will show, their efforts gave added prominence to the difficulties inherent in empirical psychology.

An awareness of these difficulties was not, however, dependent on a familiarity with Berkeley and Hume. It appears in popular philosophy at least as early as the *Characteristicks* of Lord Shaftesbury (1711), who wrote primarily in response to Hobbes and Locke.[8] To Locke's concept of the self as subject to its experience, and to Hobbes's scepticism about the dignity of human nature, Shaftesbury opposes a belief in the self's native aspiration to the beautiful and good, a belief that is largely inspired by Platonic and Stoic philosophy. Yet in developing and supporting his theories, Shaftesbury appeals to the empirical evidence of immediate perception and personal experience.[9] He tries to fight Hobbes and Locke on their own ground, and in doing so he involves himself in many of the perplexities that other eighteenth-century thinkers were to encounter in attempting to develop a satisfactory concept of the self.

Shaftesbury is a master at making philosophical problems look easy to solve, but he is forced to admit that he cannot explain how the self can be sure that the outside world exists: "All which even *Sense* suggests may be deceitful."[10] He insists, however, that "we cannot doubt of what passes *within ourselves*. Our Passions and Affections are known to us. *They* are certain, whatever the *Objects* may be, on which they are employ'd." Although Shaftesbury tries to ignore the problem of solipsism that he has raised, his recognition that it exists makes him, for a moment, somewhat wistful: "Nor is it of any concern to our Argument, how . . . exterior Objects stand; whether they are Realitys, or mere Illusions; whether we wake or dream. For *ill Dreams* will be equally disturbing. And a good *Dream* (if Life be nothing else) will be easily and happily pass'd."[11]

"If Life be nothing else. . . ." This hesitancy about the ultimate value of human life has its counterpart in the works of Hume, who observes with delicate irony that "the artifice of nature . . . has happily deceived us into an opinion, that human life is of some importance."[12] Shaftesbury's general solution to the problem of personal significance involves the idea that the individual self is of great inherent worth and that it can discover its value by means of a philosophically disciplined introspection: "As I am less led or betray'd by *Fancy* to an Esteem of what depends on *others;* I am the more fix'd in the Esteem of what depends on *my-self* alone. And if I have once gain'd the *Taste* of Liberty, I shall easily understand the force of this Reasoning, and know both my *true* Self and Interest."[13]

But Shaftesbury has considerable difficulty in discussing the question of personal identity with which the question of personal significance is so closely allied. He declares that we can be sure of nothing until we are sure of what the self is; but he dismisses the idea that either memory or consciousness is the basis of identity. Finding no other basis, he announces that "for my own part, I take my Being *upon Trust*." He then, typically, launches into a consideration of the moral imperative: "Who and What *I ought to be*."[14] Shaftesbury prefers to examine only the self's *moral* identity — or, rather, identities; for if there is a "true Self," there must also be what Shaftesbury calls in his private meditations "a wrong self, a nothing, a lie."[15] The true self alone is the basis of one's personal significance, but how can it be distinguished from the false? And if the two selves conflict, how can a person be "warranted," as Shaftesbury puts it, "*one and the same* Person to day as yesterday, and to morrow as to day"?[16]

His solution to this problem makes him the founder of the so-called Moral Sense school of philosophy. He argues that everyone's experience indicates that the human mind must possess inherent faculties that instinctively determine the difference between right and wrong. In fact, it is "impossible to conceive, that a rational Creature . . . receiving into his Mind the Images or Representations of Justice, Generosity, Gratitude, or other Virtue, shou'd have no *Liking* of these, or *Dislike* of their contrarys."[17] What Shaftesbury means by the true self is the "character" one constantly maintains by exercising the moral sense.

The self, then, has the innate capacity to give the "Images" of perception a morally meaningful form. Shaftesbury attempts to enhance the significance of the individual self by conferring absolute authority upon some of its internal processes. But he is anxious to avoid the possibility that one's moral perceptions might turn out to be purely subjective and idiosyncratic. After all, the self's moral significance can normally be measured only in a social context. And despite Shaftesbury's reluctance to base his self-esteem on "what depends on *others*," he is too good an empiricist to ignore the fact that people do, quite naturally, value themselves on the basis of their relations with other people. Therefore, of all the innate impulses that constitute the moral sense, Shaftesbury most emphasizes those instincts that tend to unite the self with society. Shaftesbury's idea of the true self is often difficult to distinguish from a concept of the social self. He observes, for instance, that

a Life without *natural Affection, Friendship,* or *Sociableness,* wou'd be found a wretched one, were it to be try'd. 'Tis as these Feelings and Affections are intrinsecally [*sic*] valuable and worthy, that *Self-Interest* is to be rated and esteem'd. A Man is by nothing so much *himself,* as by his *Temper,* and *the Character of his Passions and Affections.* If he loses what is manly and worthy in these, he is as much lost to himself as when he loses his Memory and Understanding.[18]

The self, then, acquires moral significance primarily through its social impulses, and Shaftesbury is so concerned with the question of moral significance that he fails to deal adequately with the equally important question of identity. His model of the self tells us a great deal about the ways in which good men are alike, but very little about the ways in which they may differ. If moral judgment is not simply idiosyncratic, if the moral sense really tells much the same thing to everyone who heeds it, then one true self must be very similar to another. Like many thinkers before and since, Shaftesbury is mainly concerned with a self that reflects the highest potential of human nature. Lionel Trilling, commenting on similar conceptions of a "best self," has asked:

Is it not the best self of mankind in general, rather than of me in particular? And if it can be called mine in any sense, if, because it is mankind's best self, it must therefore be my best self, surely its being that exactly means it isn't (as Keats called it) my sole self: I know that it coexists with another self which is less good in the public moral way but which, by very reason of its culpability, might be regarded as more peculiarly mine.[19]

For Shaftesbury, of course, this would probably be another version of the "wrong self." He is not entirely uninterested in the distinctive identities of different people; he allows that "it might be agreeable, one wou'd think, to inquire . . . into the different *Tunings* of the

Passions, the various Mixtures and Allays by which Men become so different from one another." Yet he does not so inquire; he limits himself to regretting that men, unlike bees and ants, are not uniformly steadfast in their social affections.[20]

Such naive observations have made Shaftesbury eminently vulnerable to his critics. But his treatment of the concept of self is instructive, if only because it demonstrates the ease with which an attempt to define the inner nature of the self may develop into an attempt to stipulate its proper relationship to society. Eighteenth-century philosophers increasingly recognized the difficulty of determining either the nature or the significance of the self without considering all the complexities of its relationship to the outside world. For many, the problems inherent in empiricist theories of sensation became the crucial issue. Lord Kames, for instance, in his *Essays on the Principles of Morality and Natural Religion* (1751), insists that it is impossible to regard the self as merely a series of perceptions of the outside world: "Had we no original impressions but those of the external senses, . . . we never could have any consciousness of *self*; because such consciousness cannot arise from any external sense."[21] Yet any attempt to conceive of the self in isolation from the outside world is dangerous; solipsism can destroy a person's sense of his own being:

If we can be prevailed upon, to doubt of the reality of external objects, the next step will be, to doubt of what passes in our own minds, of the reality of our ideas and perceptions. For we have not a stronger consciousness, nor a clearer conviction of the one, than of the other. And the last step will be, to doubt of our own existence.[22]

Ideally, something might be found in the very way in which the self responds to its perceptions that could provide assurance both of the self's existence and of its ability to gain objective knowledge of its situation in the world. This is the approach of the Common Sense school of philosophy, whose most influential representatives were Thomas Reid, an acute and methodical thinker, and James Beattie, a poet, professor, and irascible controversialist. In their writings, the problems of the self that arise in empirical psychology assume the utmost moral importance. Beattie explains the intensity of his desire to prove that the self is more than a series of impressions when he asserts, in his highly popular *Essay on Truth* (1770), that "to a man who doubts the individuality or identity of his own mind, virtue, truth, religion, good and evil, hope and fear, are absolutely nothing."[23] Both Reid and Beattie are alarmed at scepticism concerning either the existence of a continuous, responsible self or the self's ability to perceive the external world objectively. Such scepticism, they fear, will endanger religion and social morality, and, along with them, the self's ability to determine its moral significance. Belief in a central self must be maintained; one must not yield to the notion that the self really consists of whatever perceptions have happened to exert an influence upon it, for in that case, all values may be destroyed. Suppose that sceptical ideas about the self are accepted: what then, Beattie exclaims, will have become of the "wonders of intellectual energy, the immortal beauties of truth and virtue, and the triumphs of a good conscience!"[24] In the history of philosophy, a defense of the self has not always been considered inseparable from a defense of moral values, but in the eighteenth century the two issues were becoming difficult to distinguish.

Lest one assume that the only difficulties in eighteenth-century psychological theory are those made explicit by the radical empiricism of Berkeley and Hume, Thomas Reid emphasizes the fact that the profound paradoxes of those philosophers are implicit in the plausible, Lockean method of analyzing the self by analyzing the ideas it derives from its perceptions. In the dedication to his *Inquiry into the Human Mind, on the Principles of Common Sense* (1764), Reid writes:

The ingenious [Hume], upon the principles of Locke, who was no sceptic, hath built a system of scepticism, which leaves no ground to believe any one thing rather than its contrary. His reasoning appeared to me to be just: there was therefore a necessity to call in question the principles upon which it was founded, or to admit the conclusion.[25]

But in their own way, the Common Sense philosophers are also empiricists. Reid added to the prestige of the empirical, "scientific" approach to psychology when he declared that "there is but one way to the knowledge of Nature's works; the way of observation and experiment."[26] He shared the prevalent assumption that a concept of the self must be derived from close attention to the self's immediate feelings. On the basis of their own empirical investigations of consciousness, Reid and Beattie suggest that the self instinctively knows, as it responds to its perceptions, that it is, in fact, something real and unchanging and that it is surrounded by a meaningful world. The act of perception is an act of belief, valid belief, in the substantiality of both subject and object. The existence of what might be called a "true self" is directly, intuitively known. In Beattie's words, "our judgements concerning truth" are the result of "a bias impressed upon the mind by its Creator."[27] In answer to what they regard as a degenerate tendency in modern thought, Reid and Beattie insist that philosophy return from metaphysical "reasoning" about the self to the principles of "common sense" that they believe to be inherent in the mind.

Theories of the self that made room for instinctive and authoritative mental powers were particularly attractive to eighteenth-century thinkers, perhaps because these theories seemed to impart the greatest moral significance to individual experience. They express what R. F. Brissenden has called the "deepest fantasy" of the age, the idea that individual feeling, despite its inherent subjectivity, is somehow authoritative.[28] Reid and Beattie derive the dignity of the true self from its instinctive "bias"; Bishop Butler discovers it in "conscience";[29] and Moral Sense philosophers such as Francis Hutcheson, who systematized and extended Shaftesbury's theories, believe that they can find it in a variety of innate faculties of knowledge which they call "internal senses" of taste and moral judgment.[30] The idea of instinctive but authoritative responses became important to such aestheticians as Lord Kames and Alexander Gerard, who wished to found the canons of art on principles of "experimental" psychology rather than traditional rules. Poets concerned with the individual self and its sensibility also found the idea congenial. "Thyself first, know; then love," writes Edward Young. "A *self* there is / Of virtue fond, that kindles at her charms."[31] As I will show,

Thomas Gray welcomed Beattie's theories as an answer to the scepticism of Hume; Thomas Chatterton adopted a rather advanced notion of individual conscience as the supreme authority; and William Blake, whose works provide the individual self with a kind of apotheosis, employs the principles of conscience and intuition as a primary part of his philosophy of the "true man."

To mention Blake in the company of such figures as Shaftesbury, Reid, and Beattie raises a number of obvious problems. Eighteenth-century philosophy may justly be said to have created a preoccupation with the self which later found its place in Blake's works, but an extended discussion of his ideas will be necessary to determine his relation to his predecessors with any accuracy. At present, it is important to notice the variety of problems that may arise in a theory of psychology based upon individual feeling, even when that psychology is refined by the addition of instinctive principles of mind.

One of these problems is that a "true self" that operates by instinct and is, in fact, perceived by instinct may be very difficult to conceptualize. Some intuitive faculty of knowledge may, perhaps, give one the conviction that one has a stable identity and an innate significance, but this conviction is very far from being a fully developed, or even a very definite, concept of self. Another problem, of course, is that a reliance on instinct is unlikely to provide any more objective knowledge of the self and its significance than a reliance on Lockean "ideas" derived from experience. Joseph Priestley emphasizes this issue of subjectivity in his *Examination of Dr. Reid's Inquiry* (1774), in which he attacks the Common Sense philosophers for recommending "merely some unaccountable *instinctive persuasions*, depending upon the arbitrary constitution of our nature, which makes all truth to be a thing that is *relative* to ourselves only, and consequently to be infinitely vague and precarious."[32]

In Priestley's view, the philosophy of instinctive common sense leads to a form of moral solipsism, and his criticism might be applied to any attempt to gain understanding of human nature from individual and subjective experience. A heightened awareness of one's own instincts and sensibility may easily result in a frustrating awareness of one's "difference" from other people. According to

Thomas Reid, one of the major problems faced by even the scientific "anatomist of the mind" is that "it is his own mind only that he can examine, with any degree of accuracy and distinctness. This is the only subject he can look into. He may, from outward signs, collect the operations of other minds; but these signs are for the most part ambiguous, and must be interpreted by what he perceives within himself." Furthermore, Reid believes that "a little reflection may satisfy us, that the difference of minds is greater than that of any other beings which we consider as of the same species."[33] One recalls Blake's declaration: "Man varies from Man more than Animal from Animal of Different Species."[34] This general principle gave Blake and earlier prophets of original genius such as Edward Young a basis for advocating an individualistic art; but a recognition of the many ways in which people differ in thought and feeling also caused anxiety about the self-closed subjectivity of the individual mind.

What so many eighteenth-century thinkers are seeking is a philosophy of the self that can remove this anxiety about the "difference of minds" and about the absence of a community of understanding based on objective knowledge. Because Locke's emphatic denial of innate ideas might seem to support a more extensive denial of all innateness and all inborn similarity between minds, Locke's philosophy had to be carefully qualified and corrected. Shaftesbury argues around Locke by describing the inborn principles of the true self as faculties or "affections" that develop naturally but benefit from cultivation; they are not positive concepts that simply exist, in isolation from the rest of mental experience.[35] Reid and Beattie argue that what is "innate" and common to humanity is the mind's inborn capacity to make correct intuitive judgments of what it perceives. The distinction between innate ideas and innate capacities generally seemed real enough to the eighteenth century,[36] although the distinction was sometimes hard to enforce. The middle ground of inherent "capacities" or "faculties" was difficult to define. There is a problem in the very vocabulary used to discuss the subject: "innate faculties," "dispositions," or "sentiments" simply sound a good deal less definite than "innate ideas." And to the extent that eighteenth-century theorists, out of deference to Locke, conceived of the self as acting only in response to perceptions absorbed by the senses, they were particularly ill-equipped to make the distinction between learned and innate behaviors — something that modern experimental psychology has not yet proved capable of doing in many instances. This is one reason for the complexity of problems surrounding the self in eighteenth-century philosophy and literature: the true self cannot be conceptualized simply by reference to innate dispositions; all the vagaries of its sensibility must be taken into account.

To the eighteenth century, sensibility meant many things. It was simultaneously an ethical and a psychological concept. It was used to refer both to the self's internal order of benevolent impulses and to the medium of nervous "feeling" through which the self is affected by the outside world. The eighteenth-century concept of sensibility was a peculiar conflation of ideas and attitudes whose origins can be traced to a variety of sources in moral philosophy, theology, psychological theory, and literary practice. The most influential essay on this subject is undoubtedly R. S. Crane's "Suggestions toward a Genealogy of the 'Man of Feeling,'" published almost fifty years ago.[37] In this essay, Crane discovers the origins of sensibility in the "propaganda of benevolence and tender feeling" to be found in the "latitudinarian" theology of the late seventeenth century — earlier, that is, than Shaftesbury's praise of the moral "affections." Crane's conclusions, however, are now being seriously challenged. Crane associates the sensibility movement with a belief in the natural goodness of the human heart. In the eighteenth century, this notion is often, but not always, connected with "sensibility"; indeed, the difficulty of determining the self's moral significance is one of the most considerable problems in eighteenth-century discussions of experience or "feeling." But there is also the problem of Crane's specific evidence. Donald Greene has reviewed Crane's theological sources and concluded that no cause-effect relationship has been established between seventeenth-century "latitudinarianism" and eighteenth-century "sensibility"; that the good will and benevolence recommended by the "latitudinarians" are traditional religious values, not something invented by the seventeenth century; and that, in any case, the Anglican divines whom Crane discusses still believe that man is inherently sinful, not naturally good.[38]

Greene does not construct his own account of the origins of sensibility; he associates it, in fact, with the kind of "sentimental" over-emotionalism that is an unwelcome growth in many periods of literature, not just the eighteenth century. But although sensibility often encouraged the species of "sentimentality" that Greene has in mind, it was something more than an emotional tone or literary attitude, bad or good. The concept of sensibility—elusive of definition but lavish in its effects—was fundamentally important to eighteenth-century attempts to evolve a philosophy of experience, and it impinged at countless points on eighteenth-century ideas of human nature. This is the view that G. S. Rousseau advances in his critique of Crane's "Genealogy."[39] He argues that the ethic of benevolence that was one aspect of the sensibility movement was already ancient in the eighteenth century and is, besides, insufficient to account for the particular form that the concept of sensibility assumed in eighteenth-century philosophy or for its central position in the period's psychological theory. Rousseau shows the significance that the concept acquired in seventeenth-century scientific studies of the mind—studies that prepared the way for Locke's psychology by indicating that all processes of thought are ultimately dependent upon nervous feeling and sensibility.

Eighteenth-century scientific experiments provided further evidence for believing that the self can hardly be considered apart from its sensibility.[40] The opinion became popular that all theories related in some way to the self, or even the soul, ought to be supported by "scientific" accounts of sensation and passion. The *Critical Review* is merely expressing one form of this belief when it remarks, in connection with Malcolm Flemyng's *Introduction to Physiology* (1759), that "on the human organization depends the doctrine of temperaments, a most curious part of natural philosophy, and possibly the very basis of ethics."[41] Eighteenth-century philosophers who refer to the most significant mental faculties as "internal senses" may be employing a rather dubious metaphor, but the term does express one of the period's common assumptions: the idea that the self can best be conceptualized as a system of organs for receiving and processing perceptions.

Of all the concepts that are related to the central issue of sensibility, it was "sympathetic" sensibility that eighteenth-century philosophers found most useful in constructing a theory of the "feeling" self. The idea that the self is inherently "sympathetic" should not be regarded merely as the expression of a vague moral optimism, even though it, like any other commonly accepted idea, might sometimes be nothing more than a superficial notion piously reiterated. Most obviously, of course, this idea provided a basis in individual psychology for a humanitarian moral philosophy. But it also helped to provide eighteenth-century philosophers with a means of describing the self, evaluating its significance, and conceptualizing its relations with the outside world. Eighteenth-century thinkers struggling with the concept of self developed the philosophy of sympathy into a systematic explanation of human nature. The explanation, however, has its own difficulties. It might be argued, in fact, that the philosophy of sympathy merely clarifies and emphasizes the problems that the eighteenth century encountered in attempting to discover a useful concept of the self. At any rate, an analysis of the theory of sympathy may be helpful in indicating the manner in which the self was often viewed in both the moral philosophy and the literature of sensibility.

As one might expect, sympathy plays a very considerable part in the Moral Sense philosophers' attempt to assert the dignity of the self. They associate sympathy with man's native inclination to benevolence, and describe it as capable of forming a bond of intimacy among all members of society. Shaftesbury considers sympathy a basis of the "Natural Affections" that unite individuals in society, and in his opinion, "to have the Natural Affections . . . is to have the chief Means and Power of Self-enjoyment."[42] Francis Hutcheson discerns in every mind an internal sense of sympathy.[43] Thomas Nettleton places "that principle of *sympathy*" which he finds "so visibly implanted in the heart of man" at the center of ethics; a person "may justly be called morally good or virtuous, who has this sympathy or social passion, this kindness and benevolence, in due strength and vigour."[44]

But it was Hume who first provided an extensive empirical explanation of this philosophically useful principle. Hume emphasizes the fact that we can never directly experience another person's emotion; we can imagine what it is "only by its effects, and by those external signs in the countenance and conversation, which convey an idea of it." But in the process of sympathy, this weak "idea" of another's feeling can be converted, under the proper circumstances, into a strong "impression" similar to the feeling itself. If we bear a close resemblance or relationship to another person, our impression of ourself, which "is always intimately present with us," will become associated with our idea of his emotions and enliven it into an intimate impression. In fact, all people can communicate their emotions to us, at least to some extent, because all minds bear some resemblance to one another: "The case is the same with the fabric of the mind, as with that of the body. However the parts may differ in shape or size, their structure and composition are in general the same." And the process of sympathy itself produces still greater conformity: "To this principle we ought to ascribe the great uniformity we may observe in the humours and turn of thinking of those of the same nation" (*Treatise*, pp. 316–18).

In this system of mutual conformity, however, the self seems to maintain a key position; and Hume's commentators have frequently questioned whether this idea contradicts his concept of the self as a mere series of perceptions. But as Páll S. Árdal argues, Hume's explanation of sympathy does not require a belief in unchanging personal identity: "All that Hume needs in his account of sympathy is that at any particular time, when we are conscious, there should be a complex impression we can identify as the impression of our own person."[45] Hume shows that he has not suddenly been led to consider the self as something more than a "bundle or collection of different perceptions, which succeed each other with an inconceivable rapidity" by a comment he makes in discussing sympathy: "Ourself, independent of the perception of every other object, is in reality nothing: For which reason we must turn our view to external objects; and 'tis natural for us to consider with most attention such as lie contiguous to us, or resemble us" (*Treatise*, pp. 340–41). For Hume, at least, sympathy has little to do with what one might normally call self-awareness or self-affirmation; he uses it instead as evidence of the personality's dependence on society:

We can form no wish, which has not a reference to society. . . . Whatever other passions we may be actuated by; pride, ambition, avarice, curiosity, revenge or lust; the soul or animating principle of them all is sympathy, nor wou'd they have any force, were we to abstract entirely from the thoughts and sentiments of others. (*Treatise*, p. 363)

But sympathy does provide Hume with one means of evaluating the individual's moral significance. This is not because he regards sympathy — as did other, less acute philosophers — as something that is always morally good in itself. It is because he views the principle of sympathy as a major foundation of the social ethics and institutions that provide people with standards for evaluating their conduct (*Treatise*, pp. 575 ff.).

Hume's friend Adam Smith worked out the full implications of the principle of sympathy in his *Theory of Moral Sentiments* (1759). The highly appreciative reviews that greeted Smith's work demonstrate his contemporaries' willingness to believe both in his empirical method of studying the self and in the importance of the principle of sympathy. The *Critical Review* applauded Smith for being "fully sensible, that the only method by which moral philosophy can be improved . . . is to follow the practice of our modern naturalists, and make an appeal every moment to fact and experience." The "chief foundation" of Smith's system, the principle of sympathy, is "evident and unquestionable"; the idea that "sympathy, whence ever it proceeds, [must] be allowed to be a principle in human nature . . . surely, without the greatest obstinacy, cannot be disputed."[46] In the *Monthly Review*, William Rose praised Smith's "frequent appeals . . . to fact and experience" and alleged that the "principle of Sympathy, on which he founds his system, is an unquestionable principle in human nature."[47] In the *Annual Register*, Edmund Burke asserted that "the theory is in all its essential parts just, and founded on truth and nature. The author seeks for the foundation of the just, the fit, the proper, the decent, in our most common and most allowed passions."[48]

Smith starts from the usual empiricist assumption that the self is isolated from other selves by the nature of its perceptions. He insists that "we have no immediate experience of what other men feel"; our senses "never did, and never can, carry us beyond our own person."[49] Yet on this solipsistic foundation Smith erects a system that not only asserts the importance of the individual's "sentiments" but also places them in particularly close relation to the sentiments of society. He observes that a man who is isolated from society's influences and standards can have no way of evaluating himself morally or even aesthetically; he cannot develop self-consciousness; in fact, he can hardly be said to have a self at all:

Were it possible that a human creature could grow up to manhood in some solitary place, without any communication with his own species, he could no more think of his own character, of the propriety or demerit of his own sentiments and conduct, of the beauty or deformity of his own mind, than of the beauty or deformity of his own face. All these are objects which he cannot easily see, which naturally he does not look at, and with regard to which he is provided with no mirror which can present them to his view. . . . To a man who from his birth was a stranger to society, the objects of his passions, the external bodies which either pleased or hurt him, would occupy his whole attention. The passions themselves, the desires or aversions, the joys or sorrows, which those objects excited, though of all things the most immediately present to him, could scarce ever be the objects of his thoughts. (*TMS*, p. 110)

A person begins to develop self-consciousness when he notices that he evokes pleasant or painful responses from others: "We become anxious to know how far we deserve their censure or applause. . . . We begin, upon this account, to examine our own passions and conduct, and to consider how these must appear to them, by considering how they would appear to us if in their situation" (*TMS*, p. 112). Seeking to gain pleasure from others, we learn how to control our conduct and modify our character so that we may become worthy of receiving that pleasure. This process, which some modern psychologists call "decentering" the self, begins when the child learns that he must control his natural aggressiveness in order to escape retaliation from his parents and peers (*TMS*, p. 145). The process of social education develops the self's moral consciousness and eventually gives it that independent strength of ethical character that Smith most admires. Social reinforcement, however, continues to be important to the adult in maintaining a positive concept of himself. He may believe that he is worthy of praise, but if society perversely refuses it, he may well suffer extreme anxiety. As Smith concedes in his final revision of the *Moral Sentiments* (1790): "No man can be completely, or even tolerably satisfied, with having avoided every thing blame-worthy in his conduct; unless he has likewise avoided the blame or the reproach"; the greater a person's "delicacy" and "sensibility" — "the greater his worth in short" — the more likely he is to doubt himself when he is doubted by others (*TMS*, pp. 127, 122). As Smith's commentators frequently assert, he is hopeful about some people's ability to rise above the absolute need for social reinforcement;[50] nevertheless, he places strong emphasis on the social origin and support of individual character.[51]

In Smith's system, imaginative sympathy is the crucial process that allows us to break free of our native solipsism, internalize the attitudes of other people, and become conscious of our moral identity and significance. Although we are unable to empathize fully with others' passions, we can still observe in their behavior the signs of pleasure or pain, notice what seems to produce their emotions, and then sympathize by imagining what our own emotions would be if we were placed in a similar "situation" (*TMS*, pp. 9–13). If we find that we would experience similar emotions in a similar situation — if we "entirely sympathize" — then we approve those emotions; if not, we disapprove them (*TMS*, pp. 16–19). We judge our own emotions and conduct in a similar manner, by considering whether a spectator, viewing our behavior, would sympathize with us. The spectator whom we imagine observing us is Smith's idea of a conscience and, as such, ought to be conceived as impartial:

We can never survey our own sentiments and motives, we can never form any judgment concerning them; unless we remove ourselves, as it were, from our own natural station, and endeavour to view them as at a certain distance from us. But we can do this in no other way than by endeavouring to view them with the eyes of other people, or as other people are likely to view them. (*TMS*, p. 110)

As T. D. Campbell points out, the "impartial spectator" is also an "ideal spectator," in the sense that he does not represent the views of any particular outside observer;[52] and Smith gives eloquent praise to the moral order that can be achieved by each person in the development of his private feelings. Yet the morally autonomous self, the self that has its own standards and acts upon them, is a self that is painfully and laboriously created out of the individual's sensibility to the attitudes of other people in society. This social sensibility, maintaining its strength throughout life, may cause even a virtuous person to be "confounded" when he is censured, however unjustly, by other people. Reflecting upon this fact, Smith remarks that the "demigod within the breast," the impartial spectator or conscience, "appears, like the demigods of the poets, though partly of immortal, yet partly too of mortal extraction" (*TMS*, p. 131). This is a fitting image of the true self as it often appears in eighteenth-century philosophy and literature — a "demigod" seeking autonomy but shaped and limited by its sensibility.

Smith's theory is remarkably ingenious and inclusive; it accounts not only for the "social passions" but also for the private emotions involved in "self-approbation." It is true, as I have indicated, that in the *Moral Sentiments* the self can hardly be conceived apart from society; in fact, it might be said that the self acquires a specific identity by learning, through its experience in society, the means of establishing its moral significance. As in Shaftesbury's philosophy, the problem of personal significance attains more importance than the problem of personal identity. Yet the theory of society that one finds in the *Moral Sentiments* is itself based on an analysis of individual feelings, on a consideration of the self's sensibility to other selves and its varying degrees of imaginative identification with them. The social order ultimately proceeds from the impulses of individual selves. Although Smith cannot form a concept of self, much less a concept of ethics, without viewing the self in its social context, it is possible to regard his theory as an attempt to assert the significance of individual sensibility and of the self's internal order of feeling.

No philosopher is fully representative of an age, and Smith's theory differs on important points from some of the other psychological theories of his time. But in common with many other eighteenth-century philosophers, Smith combines a respectful interest in the web of feelings that constitutes the individual self with a similarly intense interest in the ways in which the self may be shaped by its social affections and sympathies. It is natural that the concepts of sympathy and sensibility should occupy a prominent place in the philosophy of an age that was aware of the necessity of accounting for both the internal and the external determinants of the self. Sympathy and sensibility can be regarded as marks of individual character: a person's identity can be described in terms of his particular habits of perception, his depth of moral feeling, or the extent to which he can identify himself with other people. And they can also be regarded as means by which the outside world conditions the self.

The different ways in which the concept of sensibility can be used certainly helped to establish its power over the eighteenth-century imagination.[53] But the ambiguous nature of the concept also makes eighteenth-century attitudes toward the self rather difficult to characterize simply. This is particularly true of some of the period's more detailed and explicit theories of the self. Hartley's associationist theory is a case in point. It describes a full cycle of the self's forms —from the initial vacancy of the unformed mind, devoid of innate ideas or character, to the specific identity acquired through experience and social conditioning, to a final state of "perfect Self-annihilation," a state that is to be attained by the exercise of social sympathy and benevolence.[54] Hartley's theory presents a coldly "scientific" structure of reasoning used to support some very traditional ideas of morality. But what precisely does he mean by this supposed annihilation of self? Certainly not the self's destruction as a thinking, or at least a feeling, creature. The phrase he uses may be misleading; his philosophy really seems to imply a strengthening of the self — an extension of its powers of feeling, a widening of its perspective, and a consequent increase in its awareness of its own significance.

Lionel Trilling has written that "when we attempt to trace the history of the self, we of course know that we are dealing with shadows in a dark land. Our predications must be diffident, our conclusions can be only speculative."[55] It is especially difficult to make valid generalizations about the many different concepts of the self proposed in the eighteenth century. It is possible to observe, however, the insistence with which most eighteenth-century thinkers attempt to find some basis for asserting the significance of the individual self and its sensibility. One should also recognize that even those theories that seem most decisively to subject the self to the influence of the external world can be interpreted as conferring upon the individual mind the ultimate ability to transcend itself. In these theories, what may strike a modern reader as an emphasis on the self's weakness and susceptibility, or as a concern for its moral and social significance to the neglect of its distinctive identity, might be taken by eighteenth-century readers as an assertion of the self's inherent power and value. Such eighteenth-century interpretations of psychological theory may, indeed, explain a good deal about the character of the period's literature and literary theory.

CHAPTER THREE

Self and the Aesthetics
of Sensibility

William Collins's *Ode on the Poetical Character* is on several
counts one of the most satisfying documents of literary history. It
manages, simultaneously, to be expressive of mid-eighteenth-
century tastes and prophetic of Romantic visions; furthermore, it is
a "sublime" ode that actually succeeds as poetry. In Collins's description, the true poetic genius (he is thinking specifically of Milton) dwells at a splendid remove from the commonplace:

> High on some Cliff, to Heav'n up-pil'd,
> Of rude Access, of Prospect wild,
> Where, tangled round the jealous Steep,
> Strange Shades o'erbrow the Valleys deep,
> And holy *Genii* guard the Rock,
> Its Gloomes embrown, its Springs unlock.[1]

If, in these lines, the landscape of genius seems unduly melancholy
and enclosed, it is nevertheless exalted, in keeping with the nature
of the poet—for as Collins conceives of him, he is an image of that
higher Genius "who call'd with Thought to Birth / Yon tented Sky,
this laughing Earth" (ll. 25–26). And within the jealous bounds of
the poet's retreat there lies "an *Eden*" (l. 62).

This is a poem that one knows where to place and how to evaluate. But what exactly is one to think of the *Ode to Pity* that Collins
published in the same volume of 1746—a poem clearly designed to
show one of the most characteristic moods of poetic genius? As-
sisted by "Fancy," the poet is to design a temple of Pity embellished
with many a "disastrous Tale" of human misfortune (ll. 25–36). The
pathetic has always been an element of poetry, and Collins is

concerned — as much as he is with anything very specific — with the inspiration for tragic poetry; but seldom has pity been given the strange power that he attributes to it. Pity's temple is to "raise a wild Enthusiast Heat, / In all who view the Shrine," and the poet himself is to succumb completely to its attractions:

> There let me oft, retir'd by Day,
> In Dreams of Passion melt away,
>   Allow'd with Thee to dwell.   (ll. 29–30, 37–39)

The *Ode to Pity* is a curiosity, by almost any standards except those of its own time. The poet's retirement from the world has somehow become the occasion of an uninhibited indulgence in sympathy — in this case a predominantly aesthetic passion, certainly, and one that is hardly represented as having any practical effect on society, but still a passion that is capable of becoming an almost erotic bliss.

The later eighteenth century has given British literature some of its most emphatic images of the isolated self: Cowper's depiction of himself as a "castaway"; Richardson's heroine Clarissa Harlowe, shut in a series of solitary rooms, with only her true self for company; the speaker of the *Night Thoughts* waking in darkness ("How happy they, who wake no more!") to meditate on death. But the literature of the period provides equally emphatic images of the sympathetic self: the men and women of feeling who populate Henry Mackenzie's novels, Ossian's shadowy procession of sympathetic warriors and maidens, Clarissa Harlowe and her almost compulsive charitableness. All of these images, of both classes, were seen and enjoyed as pure expressions of sensibility.

It is dangerous to reason by means of images, or to write literary history based on them; but to anyone familiar with the period these particular images are easily recognizable as highly representative of its central concern with the "feeling" self. The prominence of both classes of images, however, presents interesting problems. John E. Sitter has recently argued that exaltations of the isolated self by poets of the later eighteenth century exemplify a pattern of withdrawal from "social strife" to psychological security.[2] But this is only half the question: in poets such as Collins and Cowper one finds not only justifications of withdrawal but also lyrical affirmations of social sympathy. Fredric V. Bogel has suggested that late-eighteenth-century literature is characterized by an awareness of "insubstantiality" in the external world and in the self; this awareness is a condition similar to the state of "ontological insecurity" in which "the line between self and other may be indistinct or shifting, and other persons, things, or natural processes may seem as unreliable or insubstantial as the self."[3] As I have indicated, I believe that something similar to this is present in the period's philosophy and literature, and I think that it can be partially explained by eighteenth-century writers' personal and philosophical difficulties in conceptualizing the self and apprehending a structure of values in their experience. But I believe that the problem is also attributable to the very methods they employed to give the self significance and "substantiality," particularly to their attempt to exalt the individual self by exalting its powers of sensibility. It is partly for this reason that the self can be a rather perplexing concept in eighteenth-century aesthetics.

In the literature and aesthetics of sensibility, we see the early stages of development of what might be called a mystique of the individual self, a mystique that gained additional complexity in Romantic literature and persists, despite periodic attempts to dispel it, in much of the literature of the twentieth century. In eighteenth-century theories of original genius, in particular, we find evidence of a willingness to attribute an almost sacred significance to the processes of the individual mind. In his *Conjectures on Original Composition*, Young describes genius as a "Magician" who "raises his structure by means invisible. . . . Genius has ever been supposed to partake of something Divine." Once a person has managed to find this mysterious power hidden within him, Young's command is: "*Reverence thyself.*"[4] Young's primary interest is in exceptional genius, but this interest leads him to praise all "mental Individuality": nature "brings us into the world all *Originals:* No two faces, no two minds, are just alike; but all bear Nature's evident mark of Separation on them. Born *Originals*, how comes it to pass that we die *Copies?*" Original genius is, in fact, "less rare than you conceive":

"Many a Genius, probably, there has been, which could neither write, nor read."[5] Perhaps Young recalled Gray's *Elegy:* "Full many a gem of purest ray serene, / The dark unfathom'd caves of ocean bear." Since the eighteenth century, a respect for the superior powers of particular minds has often coincided with a concern for the undeveloped powers concealed in the rest of humankind.

Nevertheless, theorists of original genius usually preferred to emphasize its significance by calling attention to its rarity. In their accounts, genius has not yet assumed all the attributes of a Prometheus, but one can discover some of the origins of Romantic conceptions of the creative self in their belief that man's spiritual progress depends on the activity of a few exalted minds. In his *Essay on Original Genius* (1767), William Duff insists on the idea that "a small number only are qualified" to extend man's intellectual "empire": "To explore unbeaten tracks, and make new discoveries in the regions of Science; to invent the designs, and perfect the productions of Art, is the province of Genius alone."[6] In Alexander Gerard's *Essay on Genius* (1774), this quality is both "the leading faculty of the mind" and "the grand instrument of all investigation."[7] The presence of genius is clear evidence of the self's significance, and both the importance of genius and the difficulty of accounting for it make the individual self an intriguing object of speculation. Gerard observes that genius "is confessed to be a subject of capital importance. . . . But it is reckoned a subject which can be reduced to no fixt or general principles; its phenomena are almost universally regarded as anomalous and inexplicable." Gerard has his doubts about this, but his own lengthy analysis is insufficient to explain how either genius or different varieties of genius originate. He is finally forced to account for differences between individuals with an empty reference to "original differences in the constitution of the mind."[8] Like the other innate capacities that interested the eighteenth century, genius retains its mystery along with its power.

Reasonably enough, however, eighteenth-century theorists devote more attention to the processes of mind through which genius operates than to its obscure origins. They are concerned with the way in which such qualities as taste, judgment, and "invention" work together to make up the elusive character of genius. In the list of qualities that define the creative self, sympathy and sensibility generally occupy an important position. The "original," innovative power of genius might naturally seem allied less to sensibility than to untrammeled self-assertion, and eighteenth-century aestheticians often worried about the tendency of genius to disregard accepted principles of art or behavior. Nevertheless, the image of genius as naturally egoistic or indifferent to the world outside itself would surely have repelled them. Despite the eighteenth century's respect for a virtuous retirement from the world, a genius dwelling in self-willed isolation from the common feelings of humanity would have seemed to them an impossibility.

In any period, of course, descriptions of the creative self are likely to include some reference to sensitivity and depth of feeling. When Duff asserts, in his *Critical Observations* on poetic genius (1770), that "True Genius" is "incompatible with a cold, or p[h]legmatic constitution of mind," and that it "naturally produces a warmth and sensibility of temper," we may, if we wish, view his remarks simply as obvious things to say on the subject or, at most, as one more symptom of a "pre-Romantic revolt" against "Neoclassicism." But this would be to ignore the complex and extensive meaning that "sensibility" was acquiring in philosophy and aesthetics. It is not just the ability to be excited or "inspired" that distinguishes true genius; there is also "a delicacy and refinement in its sensibility . . . which is utterly unknown and inconceivable by the vulgar."[9] Like many other eighteenth-century aestheticians, Duff attempts to base his theories on a study of psychological experience, and he is anxious to assert that experience itself, especially when it is most intense, naturally assumes a morally meaningful form. Sensibility is therefore not to be considered merely as a source of inspiration or egoistic enjoyment; it naturally includes a high degree of social sympathy, and "such sympathy is the inseparable attendant of Genius." In discussing literary characters, Duff employs the same concept of an ideal self that he uses in defining the nature of the artist; the prescribed formula, which he finds particularly well exemplified in the works of Ossian, is for characters who attain significance by combining heroism with an "exquisite sensibility of passion and delicacy of sentiment."[10]

Duff's use of the concept of sensibility is grounded in the premise that the self neither exists nor ought to exist in isolation from other selves. He assumes, in fact, that it is sympathetic sensibility that allows the creative genius to express himself spontaneously. Because the artist possesses "an exquisite sensibility of every emotion . . . which can affect the human heart," his imagination is free to operate "by a simple volition, without any labour, and almost without any effort"; for this reason, he "has nothing else to do, in order to move the passions of others, but to represent his own feelings in a strong and lively manner; . . . we shall feel the same concern, and share in the same distress."[11] Creative impulse and audience response are completely harmonious; the self that creates and the selves that observe are naturally united by their mutual sensibility. As in so many other eighteenth-century accounts of sensibility, distinctions between the self and the external world break down; to look within the self is simultaneously to be in touch with the feelings of others.

One wonders how Duff would reconcile this theory with his emphasis on genius as a progressive force exalted by its feelings above the comprehension of society in general. But his concern with the self's sensibility to its experience can also be seen in his general theory of the origin of human differences. Duff argues that "diversity of character" is created by a diversity of "impressions" operating on different minds; like a modern sociologist, he can therefore assert that complex societies produce more varieties of character than do simple ones.[12]

Duff does not argue, however, that genius, despite its high degree of sensibility, is itself merely a creation of a person's "impressions" or experience. Few writers on original genius would have agreed with the offensively dogmatic William Sharpe, who in his *Dissertation upon Genius* (1755) argues on Lockean grounds that distinguished genius is entirely the product of education and acquired experience.[13] Yet eighteenth-century descriptions of genius, especially those influenced by associationist psychology, often tell us more about the self's ability to conform to its objects than about its ability to express anything very distinctive in its own character. Gerard's works provide some interesting examples of this. Whatever opinion he may finally have reached about the origins of creative genius, he tends to describe it as if it were a highly developed habit of selective perception. In his *Essay on Taste* (1759), Gerard supplies this image of the processes of genius:

As the magnet selects from a quantity of matter the ferruginous particles, which happen to be scattered through it, without making an impression on other substances; so imagination, by a similar sympathy, equally inexplicable, draws out from the whole compass of nature such ideas as we have occasion for, without attending to any others; and yet presents them with as great propriety, as if all possible conceptions had been explicitly exposed to our view, and subjected to our choice.[14]

Walter Jackson Bate has argued that such theories of selective perception are signs that individual sensibility was beginning to achieve a dominant role in British aesthetics.[15] This is true; but if we did not know what the early nineteenth century would make of these ideas, we might be able to see more clearly the problems involved in the concepts of self that theorists like Gerard employed. When Gerard published his *Essay on Genius*, the *Critical Review* questioned his habit of emphasizing the self's power of "associating" impressions derived from the external world rather than its ability to express something within its own specific character; the *Review* asked "whether the imagination is not sometimes illuminated by rays of genius that owe their introduction to none of the principles of association which this learned writer has so clearly developed, but are the inexplicable phenomena of that eccentric faculty of the soul, and, like the lightning of heaven, pervade by passages which no human penetration can explore."[16] In both his *Essay on Genius* and his *Essay on Taste*, Gerard calls the associative process of genius "invention" — the traditional word for conscious aesthetic choice — and it is true that in some fashion the process does express individual character. Ernest Tuveson, however, finds Gerard's magnet image an appropriate symbol of the passivity and lack of conscious volition that the eighteenth century often associated with genius; when Gerard compares the imagination to a magnet he "makes the genius a kind of glorified automaton."[17] Gerard's image of genius might be read (as he obviously intended it) as an image of power, but his emphasis on the mind's susceptibility to its impressions does not, perhaps, imply an especially "substantial" self. Certainly, Gerard describes the activity of genius less as an intense projection of self than as a spontaneous ordering of perceptions facilitated by a peculiar responsiveness to the external world:

A genius for the fine arts implies, at least, *sensibility* and *delicacy* of taste, as an essential part of it. By means of this, every form strikes a man of true genius so forcibly, as perfectly to enrapture and engage him, and he selects the circumstances proper for characterising it, and impresses them upon others, with the same vivacity, that he apprehends them himself.[18]

In eighteenth-century literature, the type of sensibility advocated by Gerard and many other writers manifests itself in a variety of ways. One often finds a self-conscious "sensibility and delicacy of taste" that is preeminently concerned with subtle feelings and complex attitudes. Yet just as frequently one finds a curious simplicity or transparency of aesthetic motive: the sublime effects of Young or Ossian, the pathetic scenes of Mackenzie's novels, seem only too explicitly designed to convey a series of single, strong emotions. In a period in which so much was written about the myriad and subtle processes of mind, this may seem a little strange. It is not sufficient to observe that much of the literature of sensibility falls short of the highest quality. This is true of much of the literature of any period; there are always some authors who are better than others, but it is still interesting to see if we can determine what may encourage either success or failure. Some of the works to which I refer are intended, at least ostensibly, to point and clarify a relatively simple moral; but again, this is only part of the answer. There are other issues to be considered as well, issues that arise directly from the premise that art is created by and directed to sensibility. Here Gerard's *Essay on Genius* may be instructive. At one point, Gerard praises the "true refinement" that is capable of "penetrating into such beauties as are most latent, feeling such as are most delicate, and comprehending such as are most complex." But in another place, he argues that the "natural appearances which are useful in productions in the arts, must always be such as are in some respect striking"; the man of genius need remember only "such appearances as have made a strong impression on the senses, as have forced attention, as have pleased taste, as have excited some passion or emotion, as have seemed peculiar and distinguishing." The artist needs to be "concerned chiefly with the resemblances of things, and these of the more sensible and striking kinds; and, in subordination to these, with their obvious contrasts, their peculiar and discriminating circumstances, and their more signal causes and effects." By contrast, Gerard argues, it is for the scientist to be concerned with more subtle circumstances.[19] Much of this, of course, is merely common sense: the artist does not number the streaks of the tulip, at least the less "striking" ones. But such ideas may provide justification for an art that relies, in Wordsworth's phrase, on "gross and violent stimulants" applied to the sensibility,[20] on effects that "strike" the senses and "force" attention. And there is a certain narrowness in such views.

But let us return to the quality of sympathetic sensibility that the eighteenth century often associated with genius. In any period, ethical values easily become aesthetic ones, and sympathy came to eighteenth-century aesthetics supported by the authority of moral as well as psychological theory. Lord Kames, in his philosophical and critical works, furnishes some of the best examples of what often seems to have been an unquestioning faith in the value of sympathetic sensibility. He believes that we cannot help being motivated by "that eminent principle of sympathy" which he terms, in an unfortunate phrase, "the cement of human society." Sympathy provides experiential proof of the self's moral significance — proof that is simply unarguable, for "we cannot help approving of this tenderness and sympathy in our nature; we are pleased with ourselves for being so constituted, we are conscious of inward merit; and this," he adds complacently, "is a continual source of satisfaction." Predictably, Kames believes that the arts recommend themselves "by inspiring delicacy of feeling" and by promoting "benevolence"; he insists that "delicacy of taste necessarily heightens our sensibility of pain and pleasure, and of course our sympathy, which is the capital branch of every social passion."[21]

Such statements may sound like so many moral clichés, but hidden among them there are some interesting notions about the powers of art and of the self. Art, Kames suggests, may offer not just an education in specific attitudes, but something more basic as well: a conditioning of those processes of feeling on which all attitudes depend. Implicit in the concept of sympathy is an idea of the self's power to assume new forms as it embraces new experiences, and Kames shows that this conception of the self is just as useful in aesthetic as in moral theory. Smith had made the sympathetic imagination a basis of ethics; Kames, in his well-known anticipation of Keats's concept of artistic impersonality, makes it a basis of creativity: genius, he asserts, is preeminently displayed in the mental "ductility" of "the writer, who, forgetting himself, can . . . personate another, so as to feel truly and distinctly the various agitations of [his] passion."[22]

Eighteenth-century claims regarding the value of sympathy were often, indeed, much more extreme than this. In sentimental literature there developed a quasi-religious mysticism — or, perhaps, a surrogate religion — grounded in the self and its responses to experience. This mysticism of feeling is evident in Sterne's famous invocation to "dear sensibility" and its divine source:

> —eternal fountain of our feelings! — 'tis here I trace thee — and this is thy divinity which stirs within me — . . . all comes from thee, great — great Sensorium of the world! which vibrates, if a hair of our heads but falls upon the ground, in the remotest desert of thy creation.[23]

Samuel Jackson Pratt's effusions on *Sympathy* (1781) provide a fair example of the extent to which writers of sensibility might go in picturing sympathy as a mystical force:

> Hail, sacred source of sympathies divine,
> Each social pulse, each social fibre thine;
> Hail, symbols of the God to whom we owe

The nerves that vibrate, and the hearts that glow;
     .   .   .   .

Whose heav'nly favours stretch from pole to pole,
Encircle earth, and rivet soul to soul![24]

Pratt is assuredly not a good poet, but in his enthusiasm for what Cowper called "each tender tie of life . . . / Whence social pleasures spring"[25] he is not very different from much better writers of his age.

The point of this literature in praise of sympathy is clear: the individual self attains moral significance to the extent that it can transcend its seeming limitations and become united — at least within the imagination's shrine of "feeling" — in a peculiarly intimate embrace with other selves. But in such poems as Pratt's, the question of the self's exact relation to the outside world becomes rather murky. These passionate assertions that universal sympathy *must* exist may well betray more than a little anxiety about the self's ability to overcome its psychic isolation, more than a little of that fear of solipsism of which A. D. Nuttall has written. There is surely an air of fantasy about Pratt's cosmic vision of vibrating nerves and glowing hearts, even though his diction implies that the union of souls is a physiological fact, that it can, indeed, be *felt* along the nerves.

This poetic concern for nerve-fibers may strike us as tastelessly clinical, but it is something very often to be found in eighteenth-century literature. Just as twentieth-century references to the "ego" reflect modern methods of conceptualizing the self, so the eighteenth-century imagery of "nerves" reflects that period's concern with the self's processes of perception and feeling. In Gray's *De Principiis Cogitandi*, for instance, the nerves appear as vital adjuncts of the soul, the carriers of the "fivefold procession" of sensory perceptions which, like mighty rivers, flood the oceanic mind. Cowper pictures even poetry as having nerves: the muse "pours a sensibility divine / Along the nerve of ev'ry feeling line." The nerves are prominent throughout Blake's poetry of the mind; his mythological characters live "in the Brain of Man . . . & in his circling Nerves."[26]

As my reference to Blake may suggest, however, the notion that "feeling" is of primary significance can be used to develop very different approaches to the self. Blake is interested primarily in the mind's internal dynamics; his eighteenth-century predecessors are often just as concerned with the mind's ability to find experience and value outside itself. Some of these writers, such as William Whitehead, appointed poet laureate in 1757, emphasize the idea that there are two kinds of "feeling," and that the self acquires significance only from the "feeling" that unites the individual with society. Whitehead's "The Enthusiast" is a lecture in anti-Stoicism, but even more in antiegoism. Although his speaker initially decides, stoically enough, to banish "the tyrant passions," he has been led to do so, it seems, by his spontaneous joy in nature and nature's "Solitude."[27] The speaker may appear happy, but he has, regrettably, withdrawn from society and into himself, thereby becoming something of a nonperson. It is, rather curiously, the voice of "Reason" that finally urges him to a higher form of feeling, that of social sympathy:

> Art thou not man, and dar'st thou find
> A bliss which leans not to mankind?
>   Presumptuous thought, and vain!
> Each bliss unshar'd is unenjoy'd,
> Each power is weak, unless employ'd
>   Some social good to gain.

The isolated self is removed from its sources of significance, and even from its sources of vitality. Besides, the speaker is a poet, and self-expression is meaningless if it lacks an approving audience: "In vain thou sing'st if none admire, / How sweet soe'er the strain." An indulgence in the higher sensibility will teach the self its nature and significance:

> Enthusiast go; try every sense,
> If not thy bliss, thy excellence
>   Thou yet hast learn'd to scan;
> At least thy wants, thy weakness know;
> And see them all uniting show
>   That man was made for man.

But it is difficult to find in feeling itself the distinction between inner and outer experience, between the private and the social dimensions of the self. Even Pratt's universal sympathy could be regarded merely as a certain type of internal experience confined to the nerves of particular individuals. Perhaps the sympathy that dignifies the self is really just an aspect of one's sensibility to one's own feelings. Duff is thinking somewhat along these lines in explaining the origin of sympathetic impulses in the "man of Genius":

> It hath been justly observed by some ingenious moralists, that those affections of the human mind which regard the species in general, and whose influence is the most disinterested, are in fact ultimately derived from those of a more private nature, which respect the individual alone. Hence it is, that from a sense of our own happiness or misery we learn to participate in the happiness or misery of others. . . .
>
> . . . we sympathize with the miseries of our fellow creatures in proportion to the sense we have of the miseries we ourselves are doomed to experience. From this sensibility, sympathy derives its existence.[28]

But what if one's own "sense of happiness or misery" is not the same as that of the persons with whom one "sympathizes"? What if sympathy functions principally as a way of validating one's own feelings by projecting them upon the outside world? As Dr. Johnson's Pekuah observes, "nothing . . . is more common than to call our own condition, the condition of life"; in its context, her remark is inappropriate, but it does represent a general truth.[29] The self may be isolated from effective experience of the external world by the very assumption that it has a particularly sensitive feeling for that world.

This issue will become important in my studies of Cowper and Blake; it is not something that Duff seriously considers. His intention is to establish the genius's broad access to experience. But Duff is concerned, much in the manner of the Romantics, with the fact that people of exceptional sensibility may become, in some ways, exceptionally alienated from the world. Although the genius may be distinguished by his capacity for social sympathy, and his productions may be expected to win the immediate sympathy of their audience, his "disposition" and "character" still set him apart from mankind, and make him incapable of forming "those bonds of attachment which render men necessary and agreeable to each other."[30] But while Duff suggests that sensibility may not always be effective in uniting the self with society, Henry Mackenzie suggests that it may be all too effective in causing the self to internalize social conflicts. In his essay on *Hamlet*, Mackenzie discovers the "basis of Hamlet's character" in "an extreme sensibility of mind, apt to be strongly impressed by its situation, and overpowered by the feelings which that situation excites." Because of Hamlet's emotional susceptibility, the terrible circumstances of his life destroyed his mental balance and "unhinged those principles of action, which, in another situation, would have delighted mankind, and made himself happy." Mackenzie describes Hamlet as a man whose melancholy sensibility causes him to feel in himself "a sort of double person." Hamlet's sensibility makes him interesting and admirable, but it apparently leads to the destruction of a stable selfhood: "Hamlet's character, thus formed by nature, and thus modelled by situation, is often variable and uncertain."[31] Sensibility may give significance to the self, but it may also make a consistent self more difficult to discover and preserve. This is a central problem in the novel of sensibility, and it is one to which I will return in discussing Richardson's *Clarissa*.

The self's readiness to internalize its "situation" implies a somewhat unpleasant passiveness before experience, but this passiveness is often of fundamental importance to late-eighteenth-century concepts of the self. In his *Lectures on Oratory and Criticism* (1777), Joseph Priestley exalts the mind's "active powers" above the passive; but the mind's ability to conform itself to the outside world is still essential to his theory of literature. In fact, Priestley believes that

since the mind perceives, and is conscious of nothing, but the ideas that are present to it, it must, as it were, *conform* itself to them; and even the idea it hath of its own extent, (if we may use that expression) must enlarge or contract with its field of view. By this means also, a person, for the time, enters into, adopts, and is actuated by, the sentiments that are presented to his mind.

. . . The more vivid are a man's ideas, and the greater is his general sensibility, the more intirely, and with the greater facility, doth he adapt himself to the situations he is viewing.

Priestley insists upon an idea that Smith also suggests: the self can determine its significance only by reference to what it knows of the outside world; in Priestley's formulation, "the mind . . . hath no other method of judging of itself but from its situation."[32]

In Priestley's view, the self conforms to the situations it finds in art as easily as it conforms to those it finds in life. Literature, therefore, can provide the self with new ideas of its significance and even, perhaps, of its identity. Like some modern critics, Priestley is intrigued by the psychological needs that shape an audience's response to art, and he observes that literature helps to satisfy its audience's constant need to enjoy "a new being, and a new mode of existence." In addition, literature provides the "secret complacency and self-applause" which a reader feels when he sympathetically identifies himself with admirable characters.[33] The ability to embrace new experience — indeed, the insistence with which the self grasps at any opportunity of "enjoying a new being" — might be regarded as a sign that the self is real and substantial: yet how stable can the self be if it is so eager to be transformed? There is a hint of the tragedy, or comedy, of vicarious emotions in which most of the citizens of modern society have at times participated. It is as if the villagers of Gray's *Elegy*, having learned to experience the pleasures of a literary sensibility, suddenly attempted to become, in their imaginations only, the Cromwells and Hampdens they could never become in real life.

The idea that the self readily conforms to its experience of the outside world is found most prominently, of course, in eighteenth-century theories of the "sublime." Partly, perhaps, because of its affinity with the principles of sympathy and sensibility, the idea that the mind can absorb — or become absorbed by — "sublime" qualities in the world around it became a commonplace of aesthetic theory. Samuel Holt Monk and Marjorie Hope Nicolson have provided comprehensive discussions of the general belief that the sublime not only expands but exalts the self.[34] It would be pointless to multiply examples of this common assumption here; but it is important to notice, once again, the eighteenth century's preoccupation with making the self appear significant, and its attempt to exploit the power of sensibility in doing so. According to Young's *Night Thoughts*, the self can discover its dignity simply by means of its response to the sublime:

> The soul of man was made to walk the skies;
>
> . . . .
>
> Nor, as a stranger, does she wander there;
> But, wonderful herself, thro' wonder strays;
> Contemplating *their* grandeur, finds *her own*.[35]

On its most obvious level, the poetry of the sublime might be described as an attempt to dramatize the self by surrounding it with stage sets of elaborate grandeur—storm scenes, battle scenes, views of the infinite starry sky. But these sets are not intended merely as static backdrops; the external scenery is meant to be internalized by sensibility so that it can become a property of self:

> How glorious, *then*, appears the *Mind* of man,
> When in it all the stars, and planets, roll!
> And what it *seems*, it *is: Great* objects make
> *Great* minds, enlarging as their views enlarge;
> *Those* still more Godlike, as *These* more divine.

In this passage, the self is represented as assimilating its experience; a little earlier, however, Young has informed us that "vast surveys, and the sublime of things, / The soul assimilate, and make her great."[36] Clearly, he is willing to have things both ways, as long as he is able to give the perceiving "mind" the mystic dignity of "soul." In any case, Young provides another variant of the common eighteenth-century idea that the self can realize its true "grandeur"— in moral feeling, in the creative process, or simply in the contemplation of nature—by destroying the barriers that separate the inner world from the outer. In this way of thinking, an "assimilating" sensibility is finally more important than a desire for psychic autonomy.

But, granted that the self has a tendency to conform to its experience of the outside world, it may still be asked: To what degree is the self really open to experience? To what degree is sympathetic identification, especially with other persons, really possible? The question of the limits of sensibility — and hence, as many writers of the eighteenth century saw it, of the limits of the self — has an obvious relevance to the limitations of aesthetic theories based on sympathy and sensibility.

The philosophy of sympathy gave little encouragement to the belief that different people can communicate with each other's feelings without restriction by social circumstances or moral assumptions. Philosophers and aestheticians who exalted the power of sympathy often emphasized the idea that we can develop real sympathy only for persons or feelings we already regard as virtuous.[37] Furthermore, it was generally recognized that sympathy cannot enable one to share directly in another's emotions; it can only help one to imagine himself in another's "situation" and then decide how he himself would feel in those circumstances. As T. D. Campbell has observed, Adam Smith, for example, tends to speak of situations, not emotions, "as *the* causes of action."[38] The sympathetic imagination with which theorists like Smith and Kames are so concerned is something rather different, after all, from direct experience of what lies beyond the self. James Beattie, who considers the "philosophy of Sympathy" an indispensable part of the "science of Criticism," describes sympathy as a matter of feeling "in some degree the pain or pleasure that we think we should feel if we were really in [another's] condition." Our sentiments may therefore be very different from those of the person with whom we sympathize; and, in fact, "with feelings which we do not approve, or have not experienced, we are not apt to sympathize."[39]

Samuel Johnson was not entirely convinced about the moral power of sympathy: "Why there's Baretti, who is to be tried for his life to-morrow, friends have risen up for him on every side; yet if he should be hanged, none of them will eat a slice of plumb-pudding the less. Sir, that sympathetick feeling goes a very little way in depressing the mind."[40] Nevertheless, Johnson agreed with some aspects of the psychological theory of sympathy; in one of his *Rambler* essays, he accepts the premise that "we readily conform our minds" to external circumstances when we sympathize with others. But since he believed that sympathy is a matter of placing oneself in another's situation, he also observed that we sympathize much more readily with people in situations similar to our own.[41] This idea is closely related to Johnson's interest in biography as a species of literature capable of telling us something immediately relevant to our own circumstances. It is also the basis on which such critics as Hugh Blair can advocate dramas concerned with characters whose moral qualities and social circumstances resemble those of their audience.[42]

There were considerable limitations, in fact, on what Blair calls "those affecting situations, which make man's heart feel for man"; and this, perhaps, may help to explain the vapid uniformity of subject-matter and emotional tone in some of the literature of the later eighteenth century. C. J. Rawson is undoubtedly correct in saying that although sentimentalism "seemingly advocated full emotional liberty," it limited itself by treating sensibility as a sensitivity to conventional moral ideas as well as to spontaneous emotions.[43] To the modern mind, that moral sensitivity often seems superficial, or unduly restrictive — although an amoral sensibility may certainly be just as limited. But whether it is actually confined by its moral assumptions or not, a literature based on sensibility may easily turn into a literature of situations rather than a literature that is really concerned with exploring the individual self and its "feelings." It is important to remember, of course, that the literature of the later eighteenth century places its emphasis on situations as they impinge on the delicate web of sensibility and are internalized by the self; in that literature we generally find something quite different in effect from the pattern of character determined by situation that Mark Kinkead-Weekes discovers in pre-Richardsonian fiction.[44] Yet an interest in sensibility may lead to a greater concern with the circumstances that "naturally" create emotion than with the individual responses of particular characters. Every sentimental play or novel, as well as many a "sublime" poem, such as the *Night Thoughts*, develops characters; but too frequently all the major roles are taken by situations. The nominal characters may react vigorously, if rather automatically, to these situations, but they never really become selves. We know *what* they feel, but we often learn very little about their distinctive *processes* of feeling.

In considering the literature of any period, it is easy enough to find examples of less than consummate art. It may be sufficient merely to notice the fact that late-eighteenth-century aesthetics, with its emphasis on sympathetic responsiveness and its tendency to associate genius with sensibility, might often lead those who adopted its principles to mistake clever manipulation of sentiments for delicate feeling. One example will illustrate the full potential of aesthetic misunderstanding: Hugh Blair's *Critical Dissertation on the Poems of Ossian* (1763). Blair uses the presence of sympathy and sensibility in the Ossianic poems to help prove that they are, indeed, what their author James Macpherson claimed them to be — the productions of an ancient "original genius." Blair admits that the "ideas" of the primitive Ossian "extended little farther than to the objects he saw around him." Yet despite this lack of intellectual complexity, his works show "the most exquisite sensibility and delicacy."[45] Ossian's sensibility consisted not merely of "a lively imagination, which first receives a strong impression of its object," but also of an unusual sensitivity to moral values: "We find tenderness, and even delicacy of sentiment, greatly predominant over fierceness and barbarity. Our hearts are melted with the softest feelings, and at the same time elevated with the highest ideas of magnanimity, generosity, and true heroism."[46] As a true believer in the philosophy of sympathy, Blair emphasizes Ossian's ability to exploit those "pathetick situations" that naturally evoke irresistibly sympathetic responses. Indeed, any reader who does not respond to *Darthula* can scarcely be considered human, for in it "are assembled almost all the tender images that can touch the heart of man; Friendship, love, the affections of parents, sons, and brothers, the distress of the aged, and the unavailing bravery of the young. . . . He who can read it without emotion may congratulate himself, if he pleases, upon being completely armed against sympathetic sorrow."[47]

Blair's essay on Ossian is an extraordinarily enthusiastic application of the aesthetics of sensibility. But it does show where "senti-mentalist" assumptions about the self may lead: to an insistence on the obvious value of a few stock situations and the necessity of an automatic response to them, to a view that literature and response to literature should express the sympathetic, social passions rather than the whole self.

This is somewhat ironic, because, as R. F. Brissenden has said, the eighteenth-century belief in sentiment and sensibility ultimately derives from the idea that "the source of all knowledge and all values is the individual human experience."[48] Basing their theories on empirical principles, aestheticians of the later eighteenth century usually assumed that rules of taste must be derived from the self's reactions to what it experiences rather than from prescriptive principles. One might expect this notion to encourage a freely experimental, subjective literature, even a frankly egoistic one. Yet the development of such a literature may have been delayed as much as encouraged by the insistence that sympathy and sensibility — often defined in subtly restrictive ways — provide both a source and a standard of effective art.

The issue of what standards may be used to establish the moral or aesthetic value of self-expression naturally becomes a very serious concern in a period when aesthetic, and even moral and religious, theories are derived from empirical analyses of individual psychology. The question of personal significance, in life or in literary expression, may easily become more important than the question of personal autonomy and individual creative power. Whether the self is only an internalization of its environment may be debated endlessly, but it is obvious that the more autonomous one conceives the self to be, the less capable of evaluating its significance one may become. As Adam Smith insisted, an unconditioned, isolated self would have great difficulty determining its own moral significance. The aesthetic value of purely original self-expression would, of course, be just as hard for anyone to determine; in fact, as Gerard observes in his *Essay on Genius,* pure originality — purely autonomous genius — might produce completely ineffective art:

Indeed though it were possible for fancy to create ideas wholly unlike to those things which men have access to observe, the attempt would prove entirely useless. The artist might amuse himself with the forms of his own creation, but they would produce no effect either on the taste or on the passions of others. Men can be touched only by ideas which they are able readily to conceive; and they can conceive only those ideas, the members of which sense has already deposited in the memory.[49]

The question of originality is always a relative one, and Gerard's argument is only relatively true; as we have often seen in the twentieth century, art so "original" as to have an almost entirely private meaning has eventually created an audience capable of being "touched" by it. This suggests one of the most important differences between eighteenth- and twentieth-century concepts of the creative self: the eighteenth century normally expected genius to provide its audience with something it was "able readily to conceive"; the twentieth more often expects genius to produce something for which its audience must force itself to acquire a taste. Yet this is where one may arrive if one works out the logical corollaries of the eighteenth-century idea of original genius; the crucial development took place as long ago as Wordsworth's declaration that "every author, as far as he is great and at the same time *original*, has had the task of *creating* the taste by which he is to be enjoyed."[50]

But there is still the problem of evaluating the self and its artistic expressions. Eighteenth-century theorists generally insisted that, despite the fact that taste and moral judgment are formed individually and subjectively, there is nevertheless, as Kames puts it, "a rule or standard for trying the taste of individuals in the fine arts as well as in morals."[51] That standard was usually derived from the study of people's "natural" and automatic, though subjective, reactions. In fact, a really authoritative standard of taste was never formulated,[52] and it is difficult to see how it could have been formulated on the basis proposed. Yet a belief in the obvious value of the principles of sympathy and sensibility was so common that it formed the basis of at least a general standard of taste; certainly, it shaped the literature of the period as decisively as any definite standard might have. And these two principles provided a very plausible foundation for such a rough standard of art: they were assumed to be principles that not only give the self inherent moral significance but also preserve it from a sterile isolation and enable it to communicate with other selves.

Northrop Frye has defined the literature of sensibility, in rather general terms, as the literature of "process" rather than "product";[53] and it is clear that the aesthetics of sensibility encouraged the appreciation of a variety of new attempts to give artistic form to psychological process: Sterne's whimsically "Lockean" method of story-telling, Richardson's studies of the self's attempts to define its identity, Gray's explorations of melancholy and sublimity, even Macpherson's odd mythology of sentiment. Yet that aesthetic's concern with original genius was tempered by an emphasis on the expression of emotions with which an audience could immediately sympathize, and it was further qualified by the value placed on the artist's sensibility to the feelings of people in general — or, perhaps, merely to their more conventional and predictable attitudes. What was lacking in all this was an emphasis on the importance of expressing the whole self freely or of voicing new values. Martin Price is correct in seeing, in the later eighteenth century, a "conception of personality" that was "altering" under the influence of an increasing exaltation of feeling.[54] Yet eighteenth-century conceptions of the self's powers were both expanded and limited by the preoccupation with sensibility. When traditional conceptions of the self are broken, new conceptions must be formed, and those based on a theory of "feeling" may be as abstract and reductive as any others.

As I have tried to show, eighteenth-century concepts of the self as a creature of feeling are highly ambiguous; they do not suggest an image of the self that is particularly assured or impressive. In reviewing these concepts, one often has occasion to recall the fact that the "failures" of "pre-Romantic" literature are usually mentioned as a sorry contrast to the successes of the more "egoistic" or "individualistic" literature of the Romantic period. Despite the somewhat forced distinction betwen literary periods on which this judgment rests (are the *Songs of Innocence* "Romantic" or "pre-Romantic"?), it does have a certain validity. But just to the extent that it is really "individualistic," Romanticism faces an especially severe problem of determining the basis of the self's significance and even of its identity. The "naked self," the autonomous self, the creature of its own "feelings" is as difficult to conceptualize as it is to evaluate. As every student of Romanticism knows, the attempt to discover just what this elusive self may be, and what its existence may mean to ethics, aesthetics, politics, the whole range of human actions and ideals, provides Romantic literature with much of its profundity and force.

Yet in attempting to arrive at an understanding of the self, Romantic writers often fell back on the general theories that had been devised by the eighteenth century, the first age to test the rival claims of Self and Other by the standards of a new psychology of feeling. The concept of self in Romantic literature frequently appears as the union of two contrasting principles: a belief in the genius and innate significance of the individual self, and a belief in the significance and power of its imaginative sympathy and its sensibility to the outside world. One remembers Wordsworth's description of a poet as a man endowed with not only a "more comprehensive soul, than [is] supposed to be common among mankind," but also a "more lively sensibility" than others possess; as a person who is "pleased with his own passions and volitions, and who rejoices more than other men in the spirit of life that is in him," and also as a person "delighting to contemplate similar volitions and passions as manifested in the goings-on of the Universe, and habitually impelled to create them where he does not find them."[55] The Preface to *Lyrical Ballads* is of course a relatively conservative Romantic document; it is very "eighteenth-century." Yet how many figures of the Romantic movement would have seriously questioned its central concern, not only with the native significance of the self, but also with its ambiguous powers of sympathy and sensibility? Blake, indeed, could never have agreed with Wordsworth on the question of the poet's sensibility to the outside world; but even Blake, who of all the greater Romantics rebelled most passionately against eighteenth-century philosophy, had great difficulty developing a consistent theory of psychology based on the concept of an essential and autonomous self.

But here I anticipate my conclusion. Each of the authors I am about to consider reveals an aspect of the problematic self.

CHAPTER FOUR

Defining the Self:
Samuel Richardson's *Clarissa*

Richardson's *Clarissa* is many things — an idealization of Christian fortitude, an astute analysis of social roles and conflicts, a drama of sexual intrigue. It is also one of eighteenth-century literature's fullest investigations of the self's attempt to define its identity and significance. It is hardly the only eighteenth-century novel that pursues this issue — *Tristram Shandy* immediately comes to mind — but no other work, perhaps, is simultaneously as serious and as profound an exploration of the self. Richardson places his characters in situations that force them to reveal the basis of their identities, to disclose the extent to which they are autonomous and the extent to which they are creatures of their social environments. In doing so, he clearly intends to assert a concept of psychic and spiritual independence based upon the expression of an essential self. Yet his sensitive account of his characters' psychology nevertheless provides a complex study of the difficulties involved in determining what the self really is.

The protracted trials to which Richardson subjects his heroine are designed to state an ideal of personal independence in the strongest terms. Clarissa finds that being true to herself means continually resisting the pressure of other selves. Her family preys upon her instinctive loyalty in order to force her to marry the repulsive Solmes, a man she can never love. Clarissa stands her ground. Lovelace, a man she obviously can love, finally extricates her from her family's malevolent embrace; he, however, attempts to seduce her and, failing that, rapes her. Well-meaning people try to persuade Clarissa to make everything right before society by marrying him, but she refuses and eventually dies with her integrity intact. She remains maidenly and pious — she is no revolutionary — but the important thing is that she has asserted her identity in direct opposition to the heaviest pressure that other people can bring to bear upon her. As Clarissa frequently insists, her ruling desire is to resist doing anything that might render her culpable in her own eyes: "for that is the test, after all."[1]

Richardson uses Clarissa Harlowe's isolation to study the process by which the individual self makes the perilous attempt to evolve its own order. Despite his emphasis on religious values, his novel, as Alan D. McKillop argues, should be read not just as a story about Christian martyrdom but as a "tragedy of personality."[2] One must agree, certainly, with Christopher Hill, that "abstraction of the individual from society is, of course, not peculiar to Richardson. It was an essential part of the Puritan tradition. The Puritan heroes wrestled alone with their God."[3] Yet although no one would deny that Clarissa's characterization draws heavily on religious tradition — "Puritan" seems too restrictive a term — it is evident that her wrestling is not so much with God as with herself. She is ultimately able to identify her own will with God's, but in her tortuous process of decision-making she often cannot rely on religion to provide a clear direction about what she should do, how she should weigh the rival claims of Lovelace, her family, and her own integrity. Until she makes her final resolution to submit happily to death, Clarissa generally feels God's distance from her. She tells her correspondent Anna Howe that she has "no guardian now: no father, no mother! Only God and my vigilance to depend upon"; and she ruefully adds, "And I have no reason to expect a miracle in my favour" (EL II, 95; SH III, 172). Indeed, she feels God's guidance mainly through the medium of her own personality, as she tells Anna:

Be pleased then to allow me to think that my motives on this occasion arise . . . principally from what offers to my own heart; respecting, as I may say, its own rectitude, its own judgment of the *fit* and the *unfit*; as I would, without study, answer *for* myself *to* myself, in the *first* place; to [Lovelace], and to the *world*, in the *second* only. Principles that *are* in my mind; that I *found* there; implanted, no doubt, by the first gracious Planter . . . *impel* me, as I may say, to act up to them. (EL II, 306; SH IV, 102–03)

This declaration of autonomy tells us a good deal about Clarissa's beliefs, and about Richardson's. To determine her values, Clarissa must look within herself and respond "without study" to what she finds there. The issue of whether she will succeed in asserting her identity is in itself a moral issue, because her true identity is essentially moral — it is based on moral principles "implanted" in her mind. By acting on these fixed principles, she can discover an intransigent identity and an unchallengeable sense of personal significance.

Such ideas, of course, were by no means uncommon in the eighteenth century. The image that Richardson suggests of the mind retiring into its own recesses to meditate upon itself has many parallels in eighteenth-century philosophy and literature. In *The Self Observed*, Morris Golden writes, "Wherever we look in the period, we are reminded that its guiding epistemological concept is Locke's divided mind, one part operating on signals from without and one observing these operations." Golden associates this distinction between the reflecting self and the feeling, acting self with further distinctions between "the real and the fanciful . . . the public and the private . . . civilization and barbarism."[4] But it ought to be emphasized that the eighteenth century developed many different ways of viewing the contrasting aspects of the self. In eighteenth-century moral theory, we frequently find the notion of a divided self, one part of which is assigned the duty of judging and if necessary repressing the activities of the other aspects of personality; but the controlling aspect of the mind is sometimes identified with reflective "reason" and sometimes with the private "feelings" of the moral sense or conscience — and sometimes, in fact, with both. Shaftesbury and Smith agree in regarding moral judgment as the product of a debate between two aspects of the self.[5] But in Smith's theory, the debate is ruled by an internal spectator whose existence must ultimately be attributed to social conditioning, while in Shaftesbury's philosophy it is governed by innate principles of feeling, principles that he allies with the social "affections" but clearly considers to be attributes of the "private self."

Richardson's views on this issue seem close to those of the Moral Sense philosophers, although, for a number of reasons, his relation to contemporary philosophy is difficult to define precisely.[6] The extent to which it may have influenced him directly is notoriously difficult to determine; his direct knowledge even of Locke's *Essay* has been questioned, though on insufficient grounds,[7] and what he knew of Shaftesbury's unorthodox religious views offended him (EL II, 59; SH III, 120). Yet in order to have been influenced by an idea as popular as that of the moral sense, Richardson would have had to have actually studied the works of such philosophers as Shaftesbury or Hutcheson no more extensively than most "Freudian" novelists have studied the writings of Freud. The general idea of a moral sense, furthermore, easily functions as a surrogate for traditional ideas of conscience, and in ethical writings of the eighteenth century the two concepts are often nearly identical. John A. Dussinger, therefore, has good reason to emphasize the relation between Clarissa's notion of inner principle and the teachings of Protestant theology.[8]

Clarissa, of course, is more than a study of its heroine's conscience: it is a novel concerned with moral principle, but it is also a novel of sensibility; and the relation of conscience to sensibility poses interesting questions. As Dussinger notes, conscience and sensibility are very frequently associated in eighteenth-century moral thought. Now, there is no reason to expect Richardson to write in the style of philosophers or theologians, and of course he does not; but the idea that conscience and sensibility are closely connected seems appropriate to his characterization of Clarissa. Throughout the novel, Richardson insists upon her peculiarly delicate sensibility; her acquaintances constantly call attention to it as a distinguishing mark of her character. In addition, Clarissa's principles of conscience — which she assigns to the "heart" as well as the "mind" — seem much more like innate "affections" or an innate moral delicacy than like fully formed and coldly definite ideas. She herself has considerable difficulty in defining these principles and distinguishing them from the rest of her mental experience, as she admits immediately after declaring that she has "found" impelling principles within herself: "I hope, my dear, I do not deceive myself, and, instead of setting about rectifying what is amiss in my heart, endeavour to find excuses for habits and peculiarities which I am unwilling to cast off or overcome" (EL II, 306; SH IV, 103).

Sensibility, however, may be regarded both as a delicate awareness of one's own feelings and as an ability to be strongly affected by
one's experience of the external world. The former meaning is especially appropriate to eighteenth-century concepts of the moral sense
or conscience; the latter is more applicable to the period's idea of social sympathy. The two types of sensibility, however, are closely related. In eighteenth-century philosophy and literature, it is often
difficult to distinguish firmly between them, and understandably
so; in life, as well as in theory, an ability to be affected in one manner very often coincides with an ability to be affected in the other as
well. If one regards the true self as something especially manifested
in its social affections, the problem becomes still more complex.
Lord Shaftesbury, like Clarissa Harlowe, is a firm believer in the
ideal autonomy of the innate true self, but he nevertheless regards
the sympathetic, social affections as primary attributes of that in-
dwelling self. For this reason, as I have suggested, he ultimately fails
to enforce his distinction between the inner self discovered by reflection and another aspect of the self that can be realized only through
social interaction. Similarly, for Francis Hutcheson, the moral sense
is intimately allied to a sympathetic "public sense" and to a "sense of
honor" that is particularly devoted to a desire for social approbation.[9] Although Hutcheson is at pains to distinguish all these senses,
their functions are really rather difficult to separate. Philosophers
who valued sympathy and sensibility were especially reluctant to
regard the social self as wholly false, or the inner, true self as wholly
unconditioned by society. The dignity of the individual self was de-
fended, but its significance was based in large part on its ability to
be affected by the outside world.

In this connection, it is interesting to notice that Clarissa Harlowe
is distinguished, not only by an exceptionally "nice" moral delicacy,
but also by a delicate social sensibility. Her family's barbarity,
which would prompt a steely indignation in anybody else, opens all
the springs of pathos in Clarissa. Few occasions, in fact, can be allowed to pass without a display of sensibility. When Clarissa suspects that she has occasioned an argument between Anna and her
irascible mother, she informs Anna that she is in "inexpressible
affliction" — and who, after all, is Mrs. Howe to *her*? (EL II, 108; SH

III, 191). Clarissa manifests the most approved forms of social sympathy: she is the industrious benefactress of the local poor, and she is fond of the idea that "a feeling heart" is the "principal glory of the human nature" (EL II, 466; SH IV, 338–39). I will consider some other examples of Clarissa's social sensibility a little later, but for the moment it is important to note that Lovelace also is — or, more properly, might have become — a person of sensibility. Much of the interest of his character proceeds from the fact that although he has never developed the moral delicacy that Clarissa possesses, he has, nevertheless, a peculiar sensitivity. Lovelace even has "acknowledged sensibilities" of the moral kind (EL II, 326; SH IV, 132). When Clarissa tells him, "The word *father* has a sweet and venerable sound with it" — thus touching one of sentimentalism's magic chords — he reacts as he ought: "I was exceedingly affected." But he still cannot permit her to "triumph"; her *"indifference"* to him is simply too distressing (EL II, 316; SH IV, 117). This, surely, is the key to Lovelace's sensibility: he must be noticed, loved, respected by other people; at all times he is intimately aware, not just of Clarissa's emotions toward him, but of everyone else's as well. His sensibility carries with it an urge for admiration, even if that admiration is undeserved. When he has Clarissa in his power, he must invite his friends to see her: "Mowbray, Belton, and Tourville long to see my angel, and will be there. She has *refused* me; but *must be present* notwithstanding." Then, mimicking the formulaic phrase of real men of sensibility throughout eighteenth-century literature: "So generous a spirit as mine is cannot enjoy its happiness without communication" (EL II, 214; SH III, 347). Their sensibility makes Clarissa and Lovelace almost absurdly sensitive to their own emotions — and, in Clarissa's case, to an overdelicate conscience — but it also makes them intensely concerned with other people's feelings.

R. F. Brissenden has suggested that in *Clarissa* Richardson is conducting an experiment in the moral assumptions of his time: like many people of the eighteenth century, Clarissa initially assumes that all men are by nature benevolent; she finds, to her cost, that they do not act as if they were.[10] I would suggest that Richardson is also, though not necessarily by conscious choice or direction, testing the validity of certain other assumptions about the nature of the self, particularly the assumption that a "true," essential identity can be found beneath the shifting currents of perception and feeling, an identity that can, perhaps, be maintained as something basically distinct from the other aspects of the self that are grounded in social experience.

The more fully Richardson examines the changing responses of his characters' sensibilities, the more complex the problem of self-definition and self-evaluation appears. Both Clarissa and Lovelace are fundamentally insecure about how, from moment to moment, the self should be regarded.[11] Lovelace is as much interested in asserting his identity as Clarissa is in asserting hers; parodying her, he tells his friend Belford: "I can justify myself to *myself*; and that, as the fair invincible would say, is all in all" (EL III, 144; SH V, 238). Nevertheless, he seems to require the sympathy, or at least the bemused toleration, of other people in order to support his preferred image of himself as an accomplished and intelligent libertine, charming even in his faults. This identity is continually challenged, however, by his sensibility to Clarissa's emotions. In his confrontations with her, he frequently finds his chosen identity shifting unpleasantly as a "true self" of moral principle judges and momentarily represses a false self:

She took out her handkerchief, and put it to her eyes.

I was going at the instant, after her example, to vouch for the honesty of *my* heart; but my conscience . . . would not suffer the meditated vow to pass my lips. A devilish thing, thought I, for a man to be so little himself, when he has most occasion for himself! (EL III, 125; SH V, 211)

According to Richardson's principles, of course, Lovelace finds it difficult to maintain a consistent identity because he perversely refuses to obey the commands of the true self. But because of the shocks continually inflicted on her sensibility, Clarissa also has difficulty maintaining a consistent perception of herself. Sometimes she has confidence in the moral identity that she has defined for herself, but at other times she feels that her identity is at the mercy of her environment. Even before the rape, which causes the greatest questioning and finally the greatest reinforcement of her identity, she frequently wonders whether she has not sacrificed that identity by placing herself in the equivocal position of dependence on Lovelace. To Anna she writes with regret of the *"former self"* now lost to her (EL II, 45; SH III, 100). In the half-frenzied scenes in which she and Lovelace play upon each other's sensibilities, she reveals how vulnerable her supposedly assured sense of identity and significance really is. In one of these episodes, she declares:

My temper is utterly ruined. You have given me an ill opinion of all mankind; of yourself in particular [Clarissa is not without rhetorical cunning]: and withal so bad a one of myself, that I shall never be able to look up, having utterly and for ever lost all that self-complacency, and conscious pride, which are so necessary to carry a woman through this life with tolerable satisfaction to herself. (EL II, 389; SH IV, 225)

It is interesting that Lovelace's sensibility is so affected by Clarissa's that he too begins to doubt himself; his sympathy for Clarissa makes him, for the moment, a divided self: "I had not a word to say for myself. Such a war in my mind had I never known. Gratitude, and admiration of the excellent creature before me, combating with villainous habit, with resolutions so premeditatedly made, and with views so much gloried in!" (EL II, 390; SH IV, 226). Lovelace is almost "a lost man." He is saved from the baleful effects of sensibility only by the entrance of one of his accomplices, who diverts his impressionable mind from the affecting spectacle of Clarissa's grief.

Despite the loss of self-esteem that Clarissa has suffered, it is quite obvious that she has not abandoned her essential moral principles and thereby become something other than "herself." But she is not always capable of defining her identity as something that is based entirely on her own principles. At times, in fact, she is seemingly incapable of distinguishing her moral identity (who she really is) from her social identity (how she appears to others). When Lovelace attempts to compliment her on her superiority to other people, she denounces him for causing a change in her identity:

Cheated out of myself from the very first! A fugitive from my own family! Renounced by my relations! Insulted by you! Laying humble claim to the protection of yours! Is not this the light in which I must appear, not only to the ladies of your family, but to all the world? (EL III, 135; SH V, 225)

The self with which she is concerned here is primarily a social self — the secure identity she once possessed as a member of her family; her ability, as judged by other people, to fulfill a proper social role. Before her family begins to persecute her, and before she escapes with Lovelace, Clarissa experiences no crisis of identity; her innately benevolent impulses are rewarded by the esteem of almost everyone around her. But when she finds herself in the predatory world of Lovelace and his accomplices, she feels her identity changing uncontrollably.

The difficulty of distinguishing the social self from the other aspects of identity is basic to the psychology of Richardson's novel. Like the Moral Sense philosophers, Richardson finds it hard to picture the true self as something that exists in isolation from the social self. Thus, Richardson stresses the idea that self-knowledge usually comes from one's experience of other people and one's sensibility to them. Lovelace faces his conscience only when he is forced to compare his conduct with that of the divine Clarissa. And it is only through her tortured relationship with Lovelace that Clarissa discovers and attempts to purge herself of the "pride" that lay hidden from her "unexamining heart under the specious veil of *humility*" (EL II, 378; SH IV, 209). It is through her relationship with Lovelace that Clarissa learns to clarify the principles on which she bases her identity. His pretended illness, she tells Anna, "has taught me more than I knew of myself" — the knowledge of impulses that are incompatible with the true self: "But O my dearest friend, am I not guilty of a punishable fault, were I to love this man of errors? And has not my own heart deceived me, when I thought I did not?" (EL II, 438; SH IV, 297–98).

But the irony is not merely that Richardson's two major characters, preoccupied as they are with their own emotions, are often forced to rely on contact with other people to learn the truth about themselves; it is also that neither can find a way to assert himself that is not simultaneously a demand for social sympathy or admiration. Both Clarissa and Lovelace seek, above all, to maintain a sense of their own significance. But it is hard to affirm one's significance in the absence of an admiring audience.[12] As Cynthia Griffin Wolff has shown in considerable detail, Clarissa needs not only an audience but also a social role that supports her self-image; her crisis of identity results when she is denied the chance to engage in the social roles she has learned to play.[13] This is by no means an unusual human problem, but it is an especially difficult one for people whose sensibilities are, in the eighteenth-century phrase, "feelingly alive" to every event in both the inner world and the outer. Because of their highly developed social sensibilities, Clarissa and Lovelace ultimately fail to decide exactly what the relationship of the social self should be to the other aspects of identity — and the failure results in death.

In order to maintain his identity, Lovelace requires especially lively feelings of social significance. Unfortunately, however, his sense of himself is based on his ability to fulfill a social role that is in fact impossible for him to attain: "I am fit to be a prince, I can tell thee" (EL IV, 162; SH VII, 197). Again — though one finds it here in a perverse form — one recognizes that feeling for the self's hidden significance that is best expressed by Gray's *Elegy:* Lovelace pictures himself as a man who might have swayed the rod of empire. There is an intentionally ingratiating irony in Lovelace's habitual comparisons of himself with world rulers, but beneath the humor lies a greedy desire for significance — as Mrs. Fortescue, who describes his character to Anna Howe, notices quite early in the novel. She cites Lovelace as saying that he "valued himself that he only wanted Caesar's out-setting to make a figure among his contemporaries," and then comments:

He spoke this indeed . . . with an air of pleasantry; for . . . he has the art of acknowledging his vanity with so much humour that it sets him above the contempt which is due to vanity and self-opinion, and at the same time half persuades those who hear him that he really deserves the exaltation he gives himself. (EL I, 50; SH I, 73)

But as he himself admits, Lovelace assuredly lacks the proper "out-setting" for heroic activity. The greatest achievement that seems to be reserved for him is to fill a seat in Parliament, as his uncle, Lord M, does — a fate that seems as dull as M's own character.[14] Lovelace despises the lack of adventure in such an existence, so he makes himself the "emperor" of a ridiculous — and boring — company of rakes. Lovelace's craving for significance, for action that can make him a person of consequence in the eyes of one audience or another, produces a peculiar disfigurement, a lack of proportion, in his personality. Despite his allegiance to the rakes, many of his ideas are as conventional as Clarissa's. He believes in orthodox religion; he is honorable in his friendships and business dealings; he is capable of recognizing the obligations, not only of duty, but of charity, toward social inferiors. All of this may not seem to fit his character as hardened libertine, but it is evidence of Richardson's insight into his conflict of identities.[15] Lovelace has a character that is potentially moral — he even has vague plans for a reformation sometime in the future — but he is unable to assert his moral identity except when he stands to gain social recognition by doing so. As the "Rosebud" incident plainly shows, Lovelace's worthy treatment of inferiors is motivated by a desire to gain respect, to be of significance in others' eyes; he refrains from seducing the girl because her grandmother flatters his ego by recognizing his power and imploring his forbearance: "This is the right way with me. Many and many a pretty rogue had I spared, whom I did *not* spare, had my power been acknowledged, and my mercy in time implored" (EL I, 170; SH I, 250).

On this occasion, Lovelace's sensibility to his inferiors' feelings is manifested in a parade of social delicacy. Yet when a conventional stage proves too narrow for Lovelace to dramatize himself fully, he is accustomed to gain significance by violating the conventions. This is the character in which we know him best — the seducer, the scoffer at authority. Lovelace's fantasy of raping Anna Howe, her mother, and her maidservant, and of then escaping unpunished after a trial before an admiring court, is a faithful expression of his frustrated desire for social significance. Yet beneath this daydream of triumphant aggression lurks a fear that he can never really feel significant, even if he can manage to make others regard him as a hero. In his fantasy, Lovelace marches to court through a crowd assembled as if for the triumph of a general or the coronation of a monarch. Yet his sense of irony recognizes the fact that the whole "*mob-attracting* occasion" depends on the attendance of the spectators who come to gape at it—the people whom Lovelace calls the *"street-swarmers,"* the "canaille" (EL II, 423; SH IV, 275–76). The identity that Lovelace bases on others' esteem is fundamentally hollow; he sees that even if he should attain the heights of the social hierarchy, his honor would still proceed from the plaudits of those he must despise as beneath him.

There is another reason why the basis of Lovelace's identity is flawed. Seeking to support his vulnerable self-esteem by sexual adventurism, he is impelled to greater and greater conquests until at last, inevitably, he meets someone he cannot rule. This, of course, is Clarissa. He desires Clarissa because she is not one of the "canaille"; because she is virtuous and resolute in addition to being beautiful, conquering her would prove his own significance. He asks his friend Belford if it has "not been a constant maxim with us, that the greater the *merit* on the woman's side, the nobler the victory on the man's?" (EL II, 252; SH IV, 23). Yet the only way he can possess Clarissa is by giving up his significance in the world of sexual adventurism, by being conquered himself by the dull life of a proper husband. As he says more than once, "What a figure should I make in rakish annals, if at last I should be caught in my own gin?" (EL II, 417; SH IV, 266).[16] It is in the "rakish" world that Lovelace has attained recognition as sexual hero, emperor of subjugated womanhood; possession of Clarissa on the only terms she will allow would demote him to a position of mild respectability in the conventional world.

At last, of course, Lovelace proves unable to conquer Clarissa and thereby use her to validate his own identity. By this time he is incapable of responding to the demands of his long-repressed true self, but he can no longer value the self based on social mastery that has crumbled before Clarissa's intransigence.[17] Previously, in forming strategies against her, he has momentarily recoiled from this false self: "But how came this in? I am ever of party against myself. One day, I fancy, I shall hate myself on recollecting what I am about at this instant" (EL II, 469; SH IV, 342–43). But although Lovelace never turns against himself with the steady loathing that Clarissa would desire, his prophecy is at least partially fulfilled.

Tortured by disappointed grief after her death, he exclaims: "And when I consider all my actions . . . I can pronounce damnation upon myself" (EL IV, 378; SH VIII, 51). Of course, he is self-asserting and self-dramatizing to the end, as when he speaks carelessly of the man who is to avenge Clarissa's death by killing him: "The meeting of twenty Colonel Mordens, were there twenty to meet in turn, would be nothing to me" (EL IV, 522; SH VIII, 265). Yet he simultaneously perceives himself as "the most miserable of beings"; he threatens to "turn hermit"; he declares that "there is no living at this rate — d — — n me if there be!" (EL IV, 522, 525; SH VIII, 265, 268). Surely it is a man who already despairs of himself who faces Morden's avenging sword.

Clarissa's struggle for identity and significance is emphatically different from that of Lovelace, because her social sensibility is always combined with a moral one. Her decision not to marry the man who has violated her is a wholly justified assertion of her true self. But what is the motive behind her willing submission to death? Naturally, one must recognize that Clarissa is a construction of Richardson's imagination rather than a real person, and that one cannot apply all the methods of depth psychology in attempting to understand her character. Furthermore, it is clear that Richardson requires her death as the climax of his Christian tragedy. But to the extent that he has explored her psychology — and that is a very great extent indeed — and has described her death as necessitated by that psychology rather than using it merely as pathetic stage machinery, one should be able to explain what impels her to death and not to other means of asserting her personal integrity.

Clarissa martyrs herself primarily because her parents' rejection and her violation by Lovelace have fatally damaged her sense of her own significance in relation to other people. Her true self triumphs in her rejection of Lovelace, but her social self, which depends on her ability to realize herself in interaction with others, has been injured irreparably. She eventually comes to believe that submission to death is submission to God's will, but she is prepared to admit that there are other reasons for her approaching death:

The strong sense I have ever had of my fault [in leaving her family], the loss of my reputation, my disappointments, the determined resentment of my friends, *aiding* the barbarous usage I have met with where I least deserved it, have seized upon my heart: seized upon it, before it was so well fortified by *religious considerations* as I hope it now is. (EL III, 522; SH VI, 412)

She concedes that although she hopes that her feelings have "obtained a better root," they were originally "*brought on* by disappointment (the world showing me early, even at my first *rushing* into it, its true and ugly face)" (EL IV, 2; SH VI, 419).

Lovelace once speaks of the fantasies that arise from either fear or desire as "the more immediate offspring of the soul," and it is a thought worth considering (EL IV, 297; SH VII, 397). As Patricia Meyer Spacks has observed, one may gain insight into the "psychic action" in a work of literature by inquiring what its characters "really want."[18] Desire is a direct expression of identity, and the fulfillment of desire is often necessary to maintain identity. Clarissa dies because too many of the fundamental desires that express her identity have been disappointed. One of her desires is the defense of those inward principles that constitute her essential self, but another is the achievement of a stable, supportive relationship with other people. This desire, the product of a lively social sensibility, is just as much a part of her nature as her individual principles. It takes many forms — above all, that of an urgent need for reconciliation with her family, something she seeks almost to the end of her life. She wants to return to the time when, she claims, she was "one of the happiest creatures in the world, beloved by the best and most indulgent of parents, and rejoicing in the kind favour of two affectionate uncles, and in the esteem of everyone" (EL I, 167; SH I, 244).

In addition to a desire for the sympathy of her family, Clarissa has a vague wish for an ideal lover, a person of sensibility, of course, "who had a tenderness in his nature for the calamities of others, which would have given a moral assurance, that he would have been still less wanting in grateful returns to an obliging spirit" (EL I, 198; SH I, 290). But Clarissa cherishes yet another desire, one that she habitually ranks above even her wish for such an ideally maidenly young man: she wishes to live "the single life " (EL I, 185; SH I, 270). This desire becomes increasingly prominent during her attempts to escape from her parents' insistence that she marry the horrible Solmes. Probably because of her family's jealousy of any assertion of an independent financial existence, Clarissa does not expatiate on the circumstances in which she would live the single life. Yet it is clear that this fantasy of a future life is not based on a desire to isolate herself from society. Even if she left her family and retired to the estate her grandfather left her, she would obey her father's orders "as to the manner I shall live in, the servants I shall have, and in everything that shall show the dutiful subordination to which I am willing to conform" (EL II, 62; SH III, 125). In retirement she would undoubtedly continue to occupy herself with the numerous charities that she had previously found so gratifying to both her moral and her social sensibility. Some parts of her sister Bella's charmingly malicious description of Clarissa's proposed idyll are probably not inaccurate: "And, dear heart! my little love, how will you then blaze away! . . . with your poor at your gates, mingling so *proudly* and so *meanly* with the ragged herd! Reflecting, by your ostentation, upon all the ladies in the county, who do not as you do. This is known to be your scheme!" (EL I, 230; SH I, 336–37).

Clarissa's various desires reveal her strong need, not just to assert her independence, but also to acquire significance in a social and moral hierarchy. She wants to maintain her own household, but only in obedience to her parents, and always with an eye to fulfilling the charitable demands of her social sensibility. She wants to marry a devoted husband, but she would judge his capacity for devotion by his virtuous sympathy "for the calamities of others." Even as an adult, she desires to fit into the hierarchical structure of her family, all the while idealizing the sorry crew. If her feeling for her mother and father were based more on personal value than on their formal position in this structure, it is unlikely, considering the injuries she has received from them, that she would persist to the end in calling these particular people her "dear," her "Ever-honoured" parents (EL IV, 303, 359, 360; SH VII, 406, VIII, 22–23). Throughout the novel, Clarissa shows herself only too ready to assert the abstract duty of children to honor their parents regardless of the treatment accorded them. Whether or not Richardson is lecturing us on his own opinions (and it is interesting that Clarissa is the only positive character who is capable of much feeling for the Harlowes), he is using as his spokesman a character who has a profound need for the support of a social hierarchy.[19]

The reward that Clarissa's social sensibility requires is what she calls "the esteem of everyone"; by submitting to all the demands of her family that she can possibly endure, she hopes to make them recognize her as a significant part of their hierarchy. In the past, certainly, Clarissa's fulfillment of all the obligations both of duty and of sensibility has given her great significance in her little world; the universal mourning at her funeral attests to her standing as a local saint. Before her troubles with her family, she appears to have derived her self-esteem quite consciously from the esteem of others: "I was the pride of all my friends, proud *myself* of *their* pride, and glorying in my standing" (EL I, 419; SH II, 263).

But when Clarissa's sensibility is deprived of its objects, it turns into something painful and self-destructive. The countless scenes in which she throws herself at the feet of her relations, trying to be allowed to rejoin the family structure, symbolize her desperate desire to buy sympathy at the cost of self-sacrifice. She evolves fantasies of suicide which she connects with the salvation of her family or the gratification of their passions. Fearing that "there will be murder" if Lovelace visits them, she declares: "To avoid that, if there were no other way, I would most willingly be buried alive" (EL I, 143; SH I, 210). She would fulfill her parents' command to prepare to marry Solmes if it only meant being "struck dead at the altar before the ceremony" (EL I, 209; SH I, 307). Painfully isolated from her father, she desires to break through to him even if it results in her death: "The wench says that he would have come up in his wrath. . . . I wish he had! And, were it not for his own sake, that he had killed me!" (EL I, 212; SH I, 310). "I, in a half-frenzy, insisted upon seeing my father: such usage, I said, set me above fear. I would rejoice to owe my death to him, as I did my life" (EL I, 430; SH II, 279).

Lovelace has fantasies of conquest, Clarissa of self-destruction, but each uses fantasy to dramatize the self. By imagining herself as a willing martyr, Clarissa attempts to reassert her right to the position in her family hierarchy that supplies her with self-esteem. Speaking to her mother, she images her will to self-abnegation in the most grandiose terms: "For, do I either seek or wish to be independent? Were I to be queen of the universe, that dignity should not absolve me from my duty to you and to my father. I would kneel for your blessings were it in the presence of millions" (EL I, 79; SH I, 115). The imaginary "millions" transform the scene of domestic squabbling into a baroque apotheosis of the self and its social sentiments. Clarissa does what many people have done in similarly distressing circumstances; she attempts to regain a feeling of personal significance by giving an exaggerated importance to her trials, even if she must do so at her own expense. Thus, she asserts that because of her own and her family's pride she has been "singled out" to be "*signally* unhappy"; she has been selected as "the *punisher* of myself and family, who so lately was the *pride* of it" (EL I, 419, 420; SH II, 263, 264).[20]

Clarissa's dream of being slain by Lovelace is a brilliant revelation of her unconscious equation of sex and death,[21] but it is also interesting as a display of her constant desire to be of significance, at almost any cost, to those around her. In this dream, Clarissa imagines that through suffering death she pays the penalty of her family's sins: "Methought my brother, my Uncle Antony, and Mr. Solmes, had formed a plot to destroy Mr. Lovelace; who discovering it, and believing I had a hand in it, turned all his rage against me" (EL I, 433; SH II, 283). Although Lovelace only makes the three offenders "fly into foreign parts," he stabs Clarissa and throws her into the grave she has been fantasizing about ever since the beginning of her troubles with her family.

Clarissa is unwilling to subordinate her true self to her social self, to marry Solmes in order to be reconciled to her family. Nevertheless, she cannot avert a crisis of identity. Lovelace's progressive "encroachments," and the eventual rape, shatter her self-esteem. During the period of madness that follows her violation, she writes: "I am no longer what I was in any one thing"; "I shall never be what I was"; "I never shall be myself again" (EL III, 205, 210, 212; SH V,

327, 334, 337). She asks Lovelace: "What is it of vile that you have *not* made me?" But despite her self-accusations, her wavering mind is capable of recognizing that she has not really acted immorally, at least in comparison with him: "Yet, God knows my heart, I had no culpable inclinations! I honoured virtue! I hated vice! But I knew not that you were vice itself!" (EL III, 208; SH V, 332). It is especially when she remembers her lost place in her family that she denounces herself:

I have been a very wicked creature . . . my sister says so — and now I am punished. So let me be carried out of this house . . . and let me be put into that Bedlam privately, which once I saw. . . .
My clothes will sell for what will keep me there, perhaps, as long as I shall live. But . . . don't let me be made a show of, for my *family's* sake. (EL III, 212; SH V, 337)

The "unworthy child" cries to her father, "My name is — I don't know what my name is! I never dare to wish to come into your family again!" (EL III, 206; SH V, 328).

In one of the short notes that she writes distractedly to herself, Clarissa reveals how deeply she has depended on an assured place in a hierarchical social structure as a means of defining and protecting herself:

Who now shall provide the nuptial ornaments, which soften and divert the apprehensions of the fearful virgin? No court now to be paid to my smiles! No encouraging compliments to inspire thee with hope of laying a mind not unworthy of thee under obligation! No elevation now for conscious merit, and applauded purity, to look down from on a prostrate adorer, and an admiring world, and up to pleased and rejoicing parents and relations! (EL III, 207; SH V, 330–31)

Clarissa seeks to define herself as an important part of a well-ordered social world. To the extent that her identity is conditioned by society, it is fragile, easily threatened; she can be happy only when she is in a protected situation between a publicly "admiring world" and publicly "pleased and rejoicing parents."[22] She regards the passions, even when they do not lead to immoral conduct, as threats to this public order, and consequently as threats to her identity. Thus, even before the rape, she tells Anna that love, if it be not *"social"* or *"divine,"* is "narrow, circumscribed, selfish"; it clearly carries "no pretty sound with it" (EL I, 135; SH I, 197). She states that if a woman in love realized "the exaltation she gives [the man], and the disgrace she brings upon *herself;* the low pity, the silent contempt, the insolent sneers and whispers," she would prefer "death itself" to the public "debasement" that love brings (EL II, 230; SH III, 371–72).

The danger of being enslaved by a man, physically or mentally, and thereby being deprived of a significant place in the social order, is one of the gravest dangers that could be posed to Clarissa's identity. This is perhaps the major reason why the rape not only causes her anguish but also makes her lose a positive sense of herself. Yet her death is not the ebbing away of a precarious vitality; as she nears it, she develops more self-assertiveness than she had at the novel's beginning. After her period of madness, she is once more able to rely upon her true self as the basis of her identity, and to rely upon it all the more because so many other aspects of her selfhood have been degraded by Lovelace. She no longer fears that she will never be herself again; she repents of various negligible sins of "pride" and imprudence, but she returns to her faith in the moral self "implanted" within her. She refuses to compromise herself by marrying Lovelace:

As to the *world* and its *censures,* . . . however desirous I always was of a fair fame, yet I never thought it right to give more than a *second place* to the world's opinion. . . . I have lost my reputation: and what advantage would it be to me, were it retrievable, and were I to live long, if I could not acquit myself to *myself?* (EL IV, 26; SH VI, 456)

Yet it is difficult, if not impossible, for any person to base his feelings about himself entirely on his own conception of his "true" nature. Even Clarissa acknowledges the strong influence of social sensibility. One of the reasons she gives for her desire to die is her inability, even if she were to lead the "single life," to endure other people's assumption that she suffered because she had willingly "run away" with a man: "What then . . . can I wish for but death?" (EL

III, 521; SH VI, 410). In the same letter in which she places integrity above "the world and its censures," she shows a strangely practical view of her family — for this reason: "And after all, what can they do for me? They can only pity me: and what will that do . . . ? For can they by their pity restore to me my lost reputation?" (EL IV, 28; SH VI, 459).

Despite Clarissa's momentary disdain for her family's pity, it is difficult to avoid the impression, whether consciously intended by Richardson or not, that much of the gratification she finds in dying is produced by the sympathy she obtains from others. She makes her suffering the center of a public drama watched over by God as well as by a large number of earthly spectators. Trapped by the circumstances of real life, Clarissa compensates by acquiring spiritual power in pathetic epistles and interviews, testamentary rewards and punishments, and letters of advice to be opened after her death. She tells Lovelace's family that she is "not without hope that he will be properly affected by the evils he has made me suffer; and that, when I am laid low and forgotten, your whole honourable family will be enabled to rejoice in his reformation" (EL IV, 92; SH VIII, 94). She uses the suffering caused by Lovelace's attempt to dominate her to ensure her posthumous power over him; she employs the threat that she will be "forgotten" to ensure that she never will be. With such psychological rewards, it is no wonder that, as she frequently testifies, her descent to death becomes a source of rich pleasure to her (EL IV, 300–03, 346; SH VII, 403–06, 459). In addition, the threat of death gives Clarissa the opportunity to become once more a part of a supportive social structure; the friends she assembles around her act as a compensatory family devoted to gratifying her need for self-esteem. Clarissa prefers to experience the form of things rather than their content — the security of knowing her duty to her father rather than the knowledge of his specific character, the ceremony of wedding a "prostrate adorer" rather than the experience of sex. She therefore finds it easy to regard Mrs. Lovick, for example, as a surrogate mother, or the Deity as a surrogate father or husband (EL IV, 213, 303, 332; SH VII, 273, 406, 449–50). To Clarissa, individuals may seem almost interchangeable as long as they stand in the properly supportive relationships to her. The problem, of course, is that Clarissa's final happiness is a flower of death, and her social rewards result from her irremediable alienation.

In *The Genealogy of Morals*, Friedrich Nietzsche argues that resignation to suffering often originates in a desire to give one's suffering some significance:

> What makes people rebel against suffering is not really suffering itself but the senselessness of suffering. . . . In order to negate and dispose of the possibility of any secret, unwitnessed suffering, early man had to invent gods and a whole apparatus of intermediate spirits, invisible beings who could also see in the dark, and who would not readily let pass unseen any interesting spectacle of suffering.[23]

Without speculating on Nietzsche's theology or anthropology, I would like to suggest that his observations on the psychology of suffering are applicable to Clarissa. Her desire to define herself in a normal social context has been destroyed, but she still requires sympathetic witnesses to her struggles if she is to be able to regard them — and herself — as significant. She disavows all dependence on her social self, but she unavoidably continues to rely on it.

Few eighteenth-century writers would have found anything strange in Clarissa's desire simultaneously to gain social sympathy and to rely entirely upon herself. As Adam Smith wrote, a person of sturdy independence will use his need for sympathy as a means of maintaining a sense of his moral identity and significance:

> He is obliged, as much as possible, to turn away his eyes from whatever is either naturally terrible or disagreeable in his situation. Too serious an attention to those circumstances, he fears, might make so violent an impression upon him, that he could no longer keep within the bounds of moderation, or render himself the object of the complete sympathy and approbation of the spectators. He fixes his thoughts, therefore, upon those only which are agreeable, the applause and admiration which he is about to deserve by the heroic magnanimity of his behaviour. To feel that he is capable of so noble and generous an effort, to feel that in this dreadful situation he can still act as he would desire to act, animates and transports him with joy, and enables him to support that triumphant

gaiety which seems to exult in the victory he thus gains over his misfortunes. (*TMS*, p. 49)

Smith might almost be writing about Clarissa Harlowe, so fully
does he describe the psychological sources of that triumphant joy
with which she faces death.

As David Daiches has written, Clarissa's victory is not "purely
private"; her death "is made into a moral victory and indeed a beati-
fication in virtue of the universal recognition of her saintliness
which it produces."[24] As Clarissa slowly approaches death, Richardson's novel gradually ceases to be a story of her inward struggles
and becomes a story of her audience's sensibility. The audience, of
course, was not just in Clarissa's death chamber; it assembled all
over England, and eventually all over Europe, wherever men and
women of sensibility felt themselves impelled to shed tears over
Clarissa's fate. There is little question, however, that in reserving
the novel's climax for Clarissa's protracted dying and the sympathy
that pours in upon her, Richardson greatly reduced the artistic
value of his novel. It is not simply that his conclusion is boring; in
fact, it is much less so than most modern readers are willing to admit
—it at least supplies the pleasure of seeing Clarissa's tormentors
punished. The basic problem is that Richardson neglects the complex issues of personal integrity and motivation that he has pursued
throughout the rest of the novel and focuses instead on the starkly
simple issue of Clarissa's death. If Richardson's portrayal of Clarissa's acquaintances reflects to any degree his judgment of mankind
in general, then it is clear that he thought people much more capable
of responding sympathetically to trials that are obvious and external than to those that are subtle and internal. While Clarissa is
struggling to decide what her identity is and how she should deal
with the pressures of Lovelace and her family, she arouses no very
intense sympathy in most of the people she knows, although her
problems do elicit a good deal of curiosity and a general wringing of
hands. But *after* the rape, the arrest, and the purchase of the coffin,
everyone—even her family—begins to sympathize with her. Her
plight is so obvious that it can hardly fail to arouse universal sym-

pathy, but by focusing so fixedly on it, Richardson converts the tragedy of personality into the tragedy of situation. Not all of his contemporaries approved of this reliance on situation; Dr. Johnson, we are told, enjoyed the first two volumes of *Clarissa* more than the last two: "For give me a sick bed, and a dying lady (said he), and I'll be pathetic myself."[25]

Clarissa, of course, is the precursor of a long line of sentimental novels in which the hero is initially isolated from society but eventually succeeds in achieving its sympathy. But for Richardson the concept of sympathy is not the ultimate solution to the problem of the self. He has as much difficulty with the problem as some of the philosophers of his time; the more deeply he studies it, the further he seems to be from proposing any single solution. Clarissa would not be who she is if she were not capable of believing that her identity is something different from the social roles she is expected to play; on the other hand, she would not be who she is if she did not require social sympathy as a means of defining herself. Richardson clearly believes that one's identity should be based on the moral principles that one discovers within one's own mind, but he cannot describe such principles as the sufficient and unchanging basis of even Clarissa's identity. He presents no stable solution to the problem of the self because he cannot escape portraying identity itself as unstable.

CHAPTER FIVE

Contexts of Significance:
Thomas Gray

The *Elegy Written in a Country Churchyard* expresses what Thomas Gray wished to believe — that the individual self is significant even when it lacks any visible signs of significance, such as power, wealth, or social recognition. Yet it was very difficult for Gray to find grounds for affirming the self. In some of his poems, he reduces human life to merely a lively consciousness of pain. In others, he finds reasons for portraying the self as significant, but his reasons are not always consistent with one another. In the *Ode to Adversity*, he bases man's significance on his capacity for sympathy and love, but in *The Bard* and "The Triumphs of Owen," on his potential for a stern heroism; in the original version of the *Elegy*, Gray describes the self as acquiring dignity through resignation to fate, but in the final version he derives its significance from the tenacity of its desires. Although Gray wrote only a small number of poems, they display a remarkable variety — a variety that resulted not just from wandering interests and a kind of aimless versatility, but also from a lifelong hesitation about how to evaluate the significance of the self.

To understand Gray's particular difficulties, it is perhaps as useful to consider what his works do not, as what they actually do, express. Compare the *Elegy*, for instance, with some other eighteenth-century poems that take up the issue of man's significance: Pope's *Essay on Man*, Young's *Night Thoughts*, Johnson's *Vanity of Human Wishes*, Cowper's *Task*. Like the *Elegy*, all of these poems recognize the self's limitations, its inability to achieve fulfillment. But unlike the *Elegy*, all of them compensate for the weakness of the self by placing it in what could be called a larger context of significance

—an order of reality that is greater than the individual experience, an order that incorporates the self and ensures its value. Some of these contexts originate in religious faith. Johnson describes the self as ultimately dependent on its relationship with God for a consciousness of its own dignity, for an assurance that it is not simply "helpless" and fated. Young, by celebrating the individual self as the most important object of God's creative and redemptive power, converts the immensity of the Newtonian universe, which might easily be seen as a threat to man's significance, into the best evidence of his dignity. Cowper suffered agonies of doubt concerning his own personal value, yet his evangelical religion enabled him to suggest a context in which the weak and obscure appear to possess the greatest importance: the humble, solitary Christian has a hidden significance in the divine plan, even though "the self-approving haughty world / . . . Deems him a cypher in the works of God."[1] But it is not necessary to propose an essentially Christian context in order to portray the self as significant: in the *Essay on Man*, Pope's consolation for the obscure sufferings of men is the argument that even human limitation is indispensable to the universe, because it enables man to fill a necessary place in the chain of being.

A context of significance provides a way, not merely of justifying the ways of God to man, but also of justifying the nature of man to himself. In addition, it furnishes a basis for discovering the moral identity of individual selves: a person can be considered good to the extent that he knows his place in the order of things. Also, and not least important, the belief that the individual's petty experience has a significant place in a greater and more rational existence is an invaluable aid to poetic rhetoric. The structure of the universe inspires the structure of poetry; no matter at what length a poet discourses on the frustrations of mundane existence, a hopeful climax, the revelation of an all-embracing order, is always available to him. For resolution he need not rely on private symbolism or purely personal emotions; he can employ the unequivocal logic of universal truth.

Gray, however, was unable to employ this positive rhetoric, because he could not affirm an external context of significance that could adequately compensate the self for its limitations. And this, I believe, could be one source of the "originality" that Samuel Johnson, writing his *Life* of Gray, discovered in the *Elegy*: "The four stanzas beginning *Yet even these bones,* are to me original: I have never seen the notions in any other place; yet he that reads them here, persuades himself that he has always felt them."[2] The passage from the *Elegy*, which describes the awkward eloquence of rustic tombstones, presents the poem's most universal statement about the nature of human life and aspiration. Having contrasted the wasted potential of the villagers with the marred achievement of the "Proud," Gray's speaker finds all people united in a common desire for their individual significance to be recognized:

> On some fond breast the parting soul relies,
> Some pious drops the closing eye requires;
> Ev'n from the tomb the voice of Nature cries,
> Ev'n in our Ashes live their wonted Fires.[3]

The four stanzas may be regarded as the climax of Gray's rhetoric, yet they are in no way consoling, at least in any conventional sense:

> Yet ev'n these bones from insult to protect
> Some frail memorial still erected nigh,
> With uncouth rhimes and shapeless sculpture deck'd,
> Implores the passing tribute of a sigh.   (ll. 77–80)

The last cry sounding from the gravestones does not compensate for the evanescence of life. As Gray reminds us, the memorials are as "frail" as the lives they commemorate. They are intended to elicit sympathy for the dead, but the most that Gray expects is "the passing tribute of a sigh." Instead of making an unequivocal declaration of the significance of human life, Gray derives comfort only from the irrepressible demand for significance. Yet by reducing his positive rhetoric to a minimum, by refusing to rely on any context of significance exterior to the self, Gray succeeds in expressing the dignity of the self's most fundamental desires in the energy with which "the voice of Nature cries" from the imprisoning tomb.

As a professed Christian, Gray might be expected to refer to the self's relationship with God as the major source of its significance.

But his belief was never strong enough to become a vital impulse in his poetry. Although one of his personal enemies, John Whalley, accused him of atheism,[4] Gray opposed "free-thinking" and considered Hume "refuted & vanquished" by his friend James Beattie's petulant attack in the *Essay on Truth*.[5] Yet in Gray's letters one looks in vain — among the weather reports, antiquarian speculations, and descriptions of landscapes — for an extended discussion of religion. It seems likely that Gray, who was himself a man of rather sceptical character, found little in what he regarded as the increasingly sceptical thought of his time that was capable of stimulating his interest in religion.[6] He sometimes used religion to console bereaved friends,[7] but any idea we may receive of his essential piety is not supported by the blank hopelessness of the epitaph he wrote for a child: "Few were the days allotted to his breath; / Here let him sleep in peace his night of death."[8]

Gray did, however, write a short essay, refuting the extreme scepticism of Lord Bolingbroke, that offers insight into his own views both of religion and of the self.[9] Bolingbroke's basic premise is well expressed in the familiar lines of his friend Pope: "Of God above, or Man below, / What can we reason, but from what we know?"[10] Bolingbroke's answer is that we have experiential evidence of God's "physical attributes" of power and wisdom, but no evidence sufficient to prove that his "moral attributes" are the same as what humans may call justice or benevolence. Gray finds Bolingbroke's philosophy offensive for two major reasons. First, by denying that there is any proof of an afterlife provided by a benevolent God, it deprives man of a comforting feeling of significance:

He will tell you, that we, that is, the animals, vegetables, stones, and *other clods of earth*, are all connected in one immense design, that we are all Dramatis Personae, in different characters, and that we were not made for ourselves, but for the action. . . . Such is the consolation his philosophy gives us, and such the hope on which his tranquillity was founded.

Gray is shocked by Bolingbroke's ridicule of a passage in *The Religion of Nature Delineated* in which William Wollaston, in a "long-

ing, lingering look behind," voices the fear of extinction at death;
Gray believes that everyone who deserves to be called human
would sympathize with Wollaston: "No thinking head, no heart,
that has the least sensibility, but must have made the same reflection."[11] According to his friend Norton Nicholls, Gray took a similarly dim view of Hume's "irreligion," "because he said it was taking
away the best consolation of man without substituting any thing of
equal value in its place."[12]

Gray's other objection to Bolingbroke is again that of a man of
sensibility whose feelings are the final arbiter of his beliefs. It is the
idea that Bolingbroke's philosophy deprives religious emotions of
their value. We could not worship God if we did not imagine that
he is benevolent, and that he exercises his benevolence toward us individually: "If we are made only to bear our part in a system, without any regard to our own particular happiness, we can no longer
worship him as our all-bounteous parent: There is no meaning in
the term."

Now, it is interesting that although Gray disputes Bolingbroke's
conclusions, he accepts his basic premise that experience is the only
source of our knowledge of God. Gray therefore argues that none of
God's attributes can be understood except by their resemblance to
our own: "How can we form any notion of his unity, but from that
unity of which we ourselves are conscious? How of his existence,
but from our own consciousness of existing?" On this basis, Gray
simply asserts his belief that God's moral attributes bear a general
resemblance to what we perceive as human virtues. We may recall
that Gray is the poet who, in *De Principiis Cogitandi*, wished to
play Lucretius to Locke's Epicurus; he is clearly enough impressed
by empirical philosophy to be convinced that all questions regarding the nature of God must ultimately be referred to immediate, individual experience.[13] But the "experience" on which Gray's religious
hopes are primarily grounded is really a fear of the psychic alienation that may result from a lack of faith in God's benevolence: "The
idea of his malevolence (an impiety I tremble to write) must succeed.
We have nothing left but our fears, and those too vain; for whither
can they lead but to despair and the sad desire of annihilation."

What evidence we have of Gray's somewhat desperate religious beliefs indicates that he was not disposed to reason very assiduously on this subject. He could find no basis for defending belief in God as anything but a projection of the self, an assertion of the self's desire for happiness and its fear of isolation. When he attempts, in his essay on Bolingbroke, to discover what may "connect" God "with us his creatures," he actually finds the "connection" only in human feelings. Perhaps he would have agreed with Emily Dickinson — another isolated self — that

> The abdication of Belief
> Makes the Behavior small —
> Better an ignis fatuus
> Than no illume at all.[14]

But it is not surprising that in his poetry Gray shows considerable reserve about presenting a religion centered in the self as the ground of the self's significance.

But religion does not provide the only context in which human life can be regarded as significant. The self can also derive its dignity from its social feelings and relations, from the sympathy it gives to others and receives from them in turn. The eighteenth century found the web of social sympathies such a useful context of significance that in many works of literature, self and sympathy became almost inseparable concepts. In Sterne's *Sentimental Journey*, Yorick's sympathy for the deranged Maria convinces him that he himself does, indeed, possess a soul. In *Tristram Shandy*, Uncle Toby and his friends are outwardly incompetent and insignificant figures; it is mainly their ability to sympathize with others that seems to give them personal dignity. As I have shown, even Richardson's Clarissa, who values herself so highly on her independence, still derives much of her self-esteem from other people's sympathy.

In the completed portion of his ambitious poem *The Alliance of Education and Government*, Gray defines man's basic characteristics as attraction to pleasure, aversion to pain, desire of self-protection — and sympathetic sensibility, the "social Smile & sympathetic Tear" (ll. 30–37). In this he shows his affinity to the empirical philosophers and aestheticians whom I have previously discussed. Yet he was seldom able to rely on sympathy as a context of significance.

This was partly because Gray's personal problems made him perpetually unsure of his own ability to gain sympathy from others. His frustrated and repressed homosexuality distanced him permanently from full intimacy with other people.[15] As if to confirm the assertions of contemporary philosophers that the self's better qualities are formed through sympathy with others, Gray — threatened by the outside world, lacking sympathy for its affairs, and suspecting, in turn, its lack of sympathy for him — looked within himself and discovered nothing.[16] Beneath his self-deprecating wit, Gray was in grim earnest when he told Horace Walpole, the idol of his youth, that philosophy had taught him that he only imagined he existed, but that "one lesson of thine, my dear Philosopher, will restore me to the use of my Senses, & make me think myself something."[17] Walpole's kindness had been "the only Idea of any social happiness that I have ever received almost"; Gray's self was "tiny" and "tiresome," but Walpole's was "large enough to serve for both of us."[18] But Walpole's kindness could never be sufficient to fulfill Gray's need for social happiness; Gray came to a full realization of that fact during their Continental tour. Years later, after the departure of Charles-Victor Bonstetten, the young Swiss student with whom he was infatuated, Gray wrote to him: "I did not conceive till now (I own) what it was to lose you, nor felt the solitude and insipidity of my own condition, before I possess'd the happiness of your friendship."[19]

But Gray had philosophical as well as personal difficulties in coming to terms with the concept of sympathy. In *The Alliance of Education and Government,* he is concerned, as one might expect from his admiration for Locke, with the issue of the self's dependence upon the outside world, but he shows that he wishes to believe that the self can attain significance regardless of the environment in which it is placed. The opposite opinion he denounces as an "Unmanly Thought!": "what Seasons can controul, / What fancied Zone can circumscribe the Soul?" (ll. 72–73). So much for the influence of literal climate, which so fascinated eighteenth-century thinkers; the poem's thesis, however, is that the self does indeed require at least an accommodating social environment in order to accomplish its full potential. And in notes that Gray apparently made for the poem's continuation, he emphasizes the necessity to the self of gaining social significance and recognition:

One principal characteristic of vice in the present age is the contempt of fame.

Many are the uses of good fame to a generous mind: it extends our existence and example into future ages . . . and prevents the prevalence of vice in a generation more corrupt even than our own. It is impossible to conquer that natural desire we have of being remembered.[20]

Education and Government was begun in 1748, about the same time that Gray was probably completing the *Elegy*; and he seems to have intended both works to express the self's desire for sympathy, even posthumous sympathy. However, in a letter also written about the time of the *Elegy's* composition, he told Thomas Wharton exactly how consoling he thought "the passing tribute of a sigh" might be:

I am not altogether of your Opinion, as to your Historical Consolation in time of Trouble. a calm Melancholy it may produce, a stiller Sort of Despair (& that only in some Circumstances & on some Constitutions) but I doubt no real Content or Comfort can ever arise in the human Mind, but from Hope. Old Balmerino [one of the Scotch Lords executed after the 1745 rebellion] when he had read his Paper to the People, pull'd off his Spectacles, spit upon his Handkerchief, & wiped them clean for the Use of his Posterity; & that is the last Page of his History.[21]

Gray's poems of 1742 reveal his inability to believe in the power of sympathy — or anything else — as an adequate compensation for the self's limitations. In the *Ode to Adversity*, written in August of that year, he attempts to use sympathy as a context of significance that can give purpose and dignity to individual suffering. He welcomes pain as a soul-maker; adversity alone can teach sympathy with others and, through it, self-knowledge:

> The gen'rous spark extinct revive,
> Teach me to love and to forgive,
> Exact my own defects to scan,
> What others are, to feel, and know myself a Man. (ll. 45–48)

But the "Sonnet on the Death of Richard West," written in the same month, views adversity—and, indeed, the soul's sensibility to its feelings—as something that isolates the self, making it incapable of sharing sympathetically in the outside world. Gray's speaker cannot share the happiness of the world around him, and he regrets that the world does not share his grief: "My lonely Anguish melts no Heart, but mine."

Gray's other poems of 1742 also admit that the self is "circumscribed," and they examine the significance of human life from that standpoint. In the *Ode on the Spring,* the speaker, who contrasts his own reclusive life with the spontaneous hedonism of the "insect youth," establishes the ultimate significance of neither: the speaker's melancholy denies him immediate fulfillment, but age will soon destroy the pleasures of the "youth." In the inverted *carpe diem* of the *Eton College* ode, the aspect of the self that recognizes its own limitations once again delivers a somber—and this time a crushing—judgment on the faith of youthful spontaneity in its own ability to achieve happiness. As Ben Jones has said, Gray has a habit of making the self's limitations almost the definition of human life.[22] In the *Eton* ode, it is the consciousness of pain that is to inform the careless youths that "they are men." This is reminiscent of the *Adversity* ode, yet here sympathy fails to provide a context of significance. The final stanza suggests praise of those who can feel sympathy, but it does not imply that they can thereby escape the full burden of human wretchedness:

> To each his suff'rings: all are men,
> Condemn'd alike to groan,
> The tender for another's pain,
> Th' unfeeling for his own.   (ll. 91–94)

It could certainly be said of Gray, as he himself said of Pope, that "no body ever took him for a Philosopher."[23] The speaker of the *Eton* ode is an image of everything that the eighteenth-century philosophers of sympathy feared—the isolated self, reflecting bitterly on its inability to accomplish anything of significance in either thought or action, incapacitated by its own consciousness from sharing the joys of others, yet regarding even its own wisdom as unprofitable "folly." In the *Adversity* ode, Gray's reliance on sympathy allows him to consider the self's interaction with its environment as something positive even when it produces pain; in the *Eton* ode, the self regards the outer world merely as something that will never respond to its own demands: "Ah happy hills, ah pleasing shade, / Ah fields belov'd in vain" (ll. 11–12).[24]

Gray's early poems, then, usually portray the self as isolated from any context in which it can achieve significance. While writing and revising the *Elegy*, however, Gray struggled to find some way of expressing a less bitter view of the human situation. In his first attempt at concluding the poem, he suggested that a kind of moral significance can be attained by resigning oneself to fate:

> Hark how the sacred Calm, that broods around
> Bids ev'ry fierce tumultuous Passion cease
> In still small Accents whisp'ring from the Ground
> A grateful Earnest of eternal Peace[.]

> No more with Reason & thyself at strife;
> Give anxious Cares & endless Wishes room
> But thro' the cool sequester'd Vale of Life
> Pursue the silent Tenour of thy Doom.

Gray's critics have usually regarded these lines as a perfectly natural conclusion, one that is highly consistent with the rest of the poem.[25]

In fact, however, nothing in the *Elegy*'s earlier stanzas, except a general melancholy feeling, adequately prepares for this conclusion. Previously, Gray has discovered bitter images in the calm that he now chooses to call consoling: the landscape abandoned to darkness, the owl complaining of intruding footsteps, the ground heaving almost grotesquely above men imprisoned forever in their "narrow cells."[26] Nevertheless, the churchyard's "grateful Earnest of eternal Peace" is supposed to resolve the speaker's conflict with both "Reason" and himself; it convinces him not to try to fulfill himself by means of either magnificent virtues or illustrious crimes. Recognizing the grateful necessity of death, he will lead a life as idly silent as the grave. Other courses are possible, but they are too morally dangerous or emotionally troubling. Yet this sort of delicate pragmatism, despite the graceful language in which it is couched, transforms a poem that seemed to be working toward some vindication of the significance of human life into a safe and rather superficial homily.

Gray was not content with his original conclusion; and in revising it, as Ian Jack has aptly observed, he transformed "a poem of Christian Stoicism" into "a poem of Sensibility."[27] Of course, even in the original ending it is only the speaker's sensibility, his feeling of a "sacred Calm" in the village churchyard, that enables him to suggest that "eternal Peace" lies beyond the grave. As in his essay on Bolingbroke, Gray resorts to feeling as a basis for the idea that man may have significance in a religious context. But in the revised conclusion he relies far more heavily on pure emotion as the basis of the self's significance. Religion is no longer associated with resignation to one's "Doom," but with a fatherly God who responds to the speaker's emotional needs by giving him "('twas all he wish'd) a friend" (l. 124). And this God, in keeping with Gray's shaky religious convictions, is kept as vague and distant as he is undemanding. The focus remains firmly on what the speaker feels, rather than on what he ought to feel; it has shifted from the duty to repress one's desires to the dignity of indulging them, even if they are melancholy or frankly egoistic. Writing to Walpole in 1747, Gray said: "Nature and sorrow, and tenderness, are the true genius of [elegies] . . . poetical ornaments are foreign to the purpose; for they only show a man is not sorry; — and devotion worse; for it teaches him, that he ought not to be sorry, which is all the pleasure of the thing."[28] In his revision of the Elegy, therefore, Gray does not suggest that it is dishonorable in the speaker (who is obviously the subject of the poem's final section) that Melancholy should have "mark'd him for her own," that he should have behaved like one who was "craz'd with care, or cross'd in hopeless love" (ll. 120, 108). Just as the passionate cry from the tomb gives dignity to the dead villagers, so the speaker's passions are intended to give him significance as well.

In the Eton and Adversity odes, Gray had offered contradictory views of social sympathy's ability to provide a context of significance and a release from psychic isolation. Now, in the *Elegy*, he hesitates. Certainly his speaker is recommended as a sympathetic person — "He gave to Mis'ry all he had, a tear" (l. 123). He warmly sympathizes with the dead, and he wishes that other people — the Kindred Spirit and the Swain — may sympathize with him when he is dead. Yet except for one friend, who is referred to but does not appear, he has apparently isolated himself from other men. One of Gray's minor revisions occurred in the line, "Ev'n in our Ashes live their wonted Fires" (l. 92), which he originally wrote, "And buried Ashes glow with social Fires." The fiery need to have one's significance recognized is surely "social," since it produces appeals to other men for sympathy. By omitting the word, however, Gray was, perhaps, not merely repressing a bit of eighteenth-century poetic jargon; he was also emphasizing the individual nature of the need and the considerable possibility that it might never be fulfilled.

The Swain's description of the speaker contains conventional allusions to the melancholy Jaques of *As You Like It*, but it is still a portrait of Gray himself. My purpose is not to psychoanalyze the poet, but I think that a letter he wrote to Thomas Wharton in 1755 expresses his characteristic attitude toward other people: "as to Humanity you know my aversion to it; wch is barbarous & inhuman, but I can not help it. God forgive me."[29] His emotions varied from haughty contempt for other people to prostrate but unfulfilled need for them, and this is well expressed by the Swain's description of a man "now smiling as in scorn, / . . . Now drooping, woeful wan, like one forlorn, / Or craz'd with care, or cross'd in hopeless love" (ll. 105–08).[30] Throughout the *Elegy*'s conclusion, Gray emphasizes the self's isolation. Originally, he wrote that the Kindred Spirit who inquires the speaker's fate was delayed in the churchyard "by sympathetic Musings"; in the final version, he is led "by lonely contemplation" (l. 95). And, more important, Gray establishes the elaborate device of distancing the speaker into the second and then the third person and presenting fragmentary views of his character in a conversation between two other people and in the epitaph on his tomb. The visitor, though a "kindred Spirit," must be imagined as having little direct knowledge of the speaker, since he is forced to inquire of the Swain about him; and the Swain's own view of the speaker is purely external. Neither of them can be expected to have any particularly intimate sympathy for him. His virtues and frailties are best known to God — and, of course, to himself.[31] The epitaph, the Swain, and the Kindred Spirit are all projections of his own imagination, offering his own evaluation of his own significance.

In the *Elegy*, personal significance does not depend fundamentally on external relationships — with God, or with other people — or on external accomplishments, even the accomplishment of reciprocal sympathy. Gray's insecurities about the world, and about himself, did not allow him to trust such solutions. Significance depends instead — somewhat paradoxically, it is true — on "this pleasing anxious being," the individual self and the emotions it feels in facing its ultimately hopeless situation. Gray no longer views human limitations, as he did in the *Eton* ode, merely as threats to the self, but as a background against which the self can display its dignity of feeling.

This change in sentiment, or at least in rhetorical strategy, affords some insight into the reason why Gray, during the 1750s and 1760s, almost abandoned the poetry of reflection for the poetry of "sublimity" and gothic terrors represented in *The Progress of Poesy, The Bard*, and the versions of Welsh and Norse poetry. Of course, one of Gray's purposes in some of these later poems was to dignify his own character as poet. This idea is supported by his conscious identification with the Bard,[32] his placement of himself in the great poetic tradition in *The Progress of Poesy*, and his choice, in "The Death of Hoel," to translate a Welsh poem in which the narrator refers specifically to his own role as elegist of his people. Also, as Donald Greene has written, Gray's interest in the gothic past provided him with "a means of escape from the real and present into a fantasy world."[33] Gray's threatened personality could be expected to enjoy compensatory wish-fulfillment, ego-involvement in glamorous situations impossible in his own unheroic life. Samuel Johnson might have been speaking of Gray's frustrated life when he wrote: "He who has nothing external that can divert him, must find pleasure in his own thoughts, and must conceive himself what he is not; for who is pleased with what he is?"[34]

But another motivation for Gray's later poetry can be discovered in his desire to represent the self as significant despite his almost morbid preoccupation with its limitations. It is important to recognize that his fantasies were usually of heroic virtue but not of heroic achievement. The world of Gray's "gothic" poems is ruled by a fate indifferent to illustrious personal qualities. In *The Fatal Sisters*, the Valkyries, pursuing their "weyward work," decide to kill or preserve without regard to personal value; they slay even men they admire:

> Low the dauntless Earl is laid,
> Gor'd with many a gaping wound;
> Fate demands a nobler head,
> Soon a King shall bite the ground.   (ll. 41–44)[35]

In the Latin text from which Gray translated *The Descent of Odin*, the mother of giants prophesies that "to the Twilight of the Gods / The Destroyers shall come."[36] In his version of these lines, Gray emphasizes and universalizes the prophecy: no inquirer will meet the prophetess again until

> substantial Night
> Has reassum'd her ancient right;
> Till wrap'd in flames, in ruin hurl'd,
> Sinks the fabrick of the world.   (ll. 91–94)

In Gray's Latin text, the prophetess foretells the death of Balder in a simple statement of fact: "Surely the divine offspring / Will be affected by pain." Gray's translation is far more resonant: "Pain can reach the Sons of heav'n!" (l. 48). The prophecy becomes the shocking declaration of a universal truth: no one, not the gods themselves, is invulnerable to fate.

In translating "The Triumphs of Owen," Gray describes a hero who is himself the agent of an indifferent fate that condemns men to "Despair, & honourable Death" (l. 36): a reflection of Gray's habitual attitude that personal virtue — "honour" — has no effect on man's destiny. "The Death of Hoel" is a more direct lesson in futility; it is in the greatest strength of their confidence and desire that Hoel and his friends are slaughtered:

> Flush'd with mirth & hope they burn:
> But none from Cattraeth's vale return,
> Save Aeron brave, & Conan strong,
> (Bursting thro' the bloody throng)
> And I, the meanest of them all,
> That live to weep, & sing their fall.   (ll. 19–24)

In some of his later poems, Gray apparently wished to suggest that poetry itself might in some way provide the self with a context of significance. Thus, in "Conan" he proclaims that memorial verse is "the Hero's sole reward" — a statement that has no precedent in the Latin text on which he based this poem.[37] And thus, in *The Progress of Poesy*, he asserts that poetry can compensate "Man's feeble race" for its limitations and thereby "justify the laws of Jove" (ll. 42–53). He apparently had a similar purpose in mind when he began *The Bard*. An entry in his Commonplace Book shows that he originally intended the Bard to prophesy "that men shall never be wanting to celebrate true virtue and valour in immortal strains, to expose vice and infamous pleasure, and boldly censure tyranny and oppression." But as William Mason noted, "unhappily for his purpose, instances of English Poets were wanting"; they had not been immortal advocates of freedom, and Gray finally completed the poem without insisting on poetry's ability to dignify mankind.[38]

Irvin Ehrenpreis has suggested that "for all its splendor *The Bard* is an assertion of its author's impotence"; its hero's suicide reflects Gray's awareness that poetry, at least in his own time, could not be an active force in human life.[39] This may be true, but it was apparently not the effects of the Bard's actions that primarily interested Gray; his major purpose was to portray a man who maintains integrity in a hopeless situation in which any action would be ineffectual. The Bard tells Edward: "Be thine Despair, and scept'red Care, / To triumph, and to die, are mine" (ll. 141–42). His victory is one of character and emotion, not of action. The doom woven in his prophecy is to deprive Edward of his queen — "to sudden fate / . . . Half of thy heart we consecrate" (ll. 97–99) — but the Bard triumphs in the sympathy of the spirit comrades whom he sees before him. As in the *Elegy*, the isolated self relies on its imagination — its vision, in this case — to provide the sympathy it cannot otherwise attain. But even after his vision has passed, the Bard's solitary strength of character continues to distinguish him. His suicide is part of his triumph — a sign of practical impotence, surely, but also a sign of moral autonomy. Gray is careful to deny the Bard any external context of significance: "Deep in the roaring tide he plung'd to endless night" (l. 144). His dignity is measured not by any hope of effect or reward, but by strength of passion alone.

Most of the other protagonists of Gray's exotic poems are also placed in situations that emphasize their independent strength of character: Odin is fearless enough to descend to "Hela's drear abode" to learn the decisions of fate, Hoel's defeat in battle provides an occasion for a friend's praise of his exceptional magnanimity, and Owen's fortitude distinguishes him in the confusion of war:

> Dauntless on his native sands
> The Dragon-Son of Mona stands;
> In glitt'ring arms & glory drest
> High he rears his ruby crest. (ll. 19–22)

The static, pictorial quality of Gray's descriptions, especially in *The Bard*, has often been noticed,[40] and this is a source of both strength and weakness in his later poems. The gothic poems are galleries of the ideal states in which Gray imagined that the self could attain its greatest significance. But the idealization is so complete, the selves represented so autonomous, so isolated from any but a purely fabulous environment, that the characters largely lack interest as personalities; they become merely heroic gestures. In order to create characters for whom one could feel an immediate emotional response, Gray chose to imitate poetry in which the self is placed in stark and desperate situations; as a result, most of his later poems lack intellectual and psychological complexity. Ironically, his characters depend for their interest largely on the extreme situations in which they are placed. He is perilously close to the practice of lesser poets of his century who relied on "sublime" stage settings to provide otherwise negligible characters with a context of significance, one that often, unfortunately, turned out to be merely rhetorical.

Anyone who attempts to analyze Gray's poetry must feel the ultimate inadequacy of any generalizations the critic may make about it. This is not only because Gray wrote a variety of different types of poetry with a corresponding variety of rhetorical strategies, or because his works are of uneven quality, or even because his finest poems can make criticism seem impertinence. It is also because his poetry lacks a central vision. His ideas are shifting, evanescent, his controlling attitude a vague *Angst*. He could seldom discern a vital relationship between the self and the outer world, yet he could not always find an effective way of portraying the self as the ground of its own significance. As a result, his view of life is narrow and fragmentary—at best, grandly pathetic; at worst, remote and sterile.

CHAPTER SIX

Self and Persona:
Thomas Chatterton

In 1769, at the age of sixteen, Thomas Chatterton submitted to Horace Walpole, the great connoisseur and the friend of Gray, certain of his works that he alleged to have been written by Thomas Rowley, a fifteenth-century priest. When Walpole detected, and reproved, the forgery, Chatterton wrote the following poem in Walpole's honor:

> Walpole! I thought not I should ever see
> So mean a Heart as thine has proved to be;
> Thou, who in Luxury nurs'd behold'st with Scorn
> The Boy, who Friendless, Penniless, Forlorn,
> Asks thy high Favour, —thou mayst call me Cheat—
> Say, didst thou ne'er indulge in such Deceit?
> Who wrote Otranto? But I will not chide,
> Scorn I will repay with Scorn, and Pride with Pride.
> Still, Walpole, still, thy Prosy Chapters write,
> And twaddling Letters to some Fair indite,
> Laud all above thee, —Fawn and Cringe to those
> Who, for thy Fame, were better Friends than Foes
> Still spurn the incautious Fool who dares— —
>
> Had I the Gifts of Wealth and Lux'ry shar'd
> Not poor and Mean—Walpole! thou hadst not dared
> Thus to insult, But I shall live and Stand
> By Rowley's side—when Thou art dead and damned[.]¹

There are at least three things of interest here. First, as Chatterton's biographer E. H. W. Meyerstein notes, Chatterton all but admits his forgery; it is no worse, he implies, than Walpole's publication of *The Castle of Otranto* as a story originally printed in the sixteenth century.[2] Second, Chatterton expresses his disgust with the sort of polite literature that Walpole writes — the "Prosy Chapters," the "twaddling Letters." Third, and most important, Chatterton makes his own claim to renown: "But I shall live and Stand / By Rowley's side."

These words are curious, to say the least, for someone who has just conceded that "Rowley" does not exist. Is not Rowley Chatterton himself? We can only conclude that Chatterton had created a persona that was indispensable to his self-esteem, one that he could not separate from his own identity — but also a persona that, to exist, must somehow be viewed as a distinct self.

This is something more extreme than Gray's answer to the question of how he had created the Bard: "Why I felt myself the bard."[3] But it is hardly schizophrenia or some "personality disorder." Chatterton is well aware of what he is doing: he knows that he wrote the Rowley poems, and he knows what resources of self-expression they opened up for him. There are, certainly, some personal problems involved in this, the problems that Chatterton suggests in his dramatic reference to himself as "Friendless, Penniless, Forlorn." He knew that his poverty and lack of education might frustrate his aspirations for a literary career, and his trials awakened in him a rankling envy and pride. In a letter of 1770 he writes:

It is my Pride, my damn'd, native, unconquerable Pride, that plunges me into Distraction. You must know that the 19/20th of my Composition is Pride — I must either live a Slave, a Servant; to have no Will of my own, no Sentiments of my own which I may freely declare as such; — or Die — Perplexing Alternative! but it distracts me to think of it.[4]

But in this Chatterton probably felt nothing that has not been felt by many other obscure and impoverished literary men. Chatterton's "Pride" is one reason for the Rowley poems, but it does not account for their specific content or for his peculiar relationship with their "author," Rowley.

The question of an author's relationship to his persona is a literary as well as a psychological one; and I think that Chatterton's choice of a persona, and his relation to it, should be seen in the context of the literature of his time and the assumptions about the self that can be found in that literature. We constantly find Chatterton trying to express himself, to make his own mark on literature; and just as constantly we find him trying to follow the cultural assumptions of the later eighteenth century. Something in the conflict or convergence of these interests necessitated Rowley.

To some extent, Chatterton must be regarded as a "naive" or at least a self-taught poet. He knew no language but English; he knew little of classical or Continental literature. But Chatterton's comparative lack of erudition makes him a particularly interesting object of study. His works provide an indication of the ideas that a young author might most easily extract from the popular literature of the eighteenth century. Describing the books in St. Bartholomew's Priory, Rowley refers to "The Booke of Tymes and Phantasies," and Chatterton notes: "The Subject of this book, is concomitant with that of a late Celebrated Piece, The Essai on the Sublime and Beautiful" — an obvious reference to Edmund Burke's *Philosophical Enquiry* into the sublime and beautiful ("The Rolle of Seyncte Bartlemeweis Priorie," *Works*, I, 144–45). Perhaps Chatterton intended to write his own aesthetic treatise, couched in his own medieval dialect; at least he was familiar with the type of aesthetic theory that was based on the self's sensitivity to the sublime. Chatterton accounts for his interest in the "Tales of Superstition" by arguing that they are more affecting than modern fables: "Let the Sentimental Reader consider, the Tales of Superstition affect the Soul with a sensation pleasurably horrid; it was Nature. Our Amusement are the gaudy Children of Fancy, we may paint clearer to the Eye but they spoke to the heart" ("Rolle of Seyncte Bartlemeweis," *Works*, I, 146). Chatterton would have agreed with Collins in the *Ode on the Popular Superstitions of the Highlands of Scotland:* "These are the themes of simple, sure effect" (l. 33). By his time, there was nothing more common than the observation that human nature is most powerfully attracted by the sublime and the sentimental.

Chatterton also adopted the conception of original genius that was popular in his time. When he sent Rowley's *Ryse of Peyncteynge, yn Englande* to Horace Walpole, he made certain to inform him that

Rowley's "Merit as a Biographer, Historiographer is great, as a Poet still greater: some of his Pieces would do honor to Pope; and the Person under whose Patronage they may appear to the World, will lay the Englishman, the Antiquary, and the Poet, under an eternal Obligation" (*Works*, I, 259). Rowley was a genius as great as Pope, and one as deserving (and as ambitious!) of fame; but it is clear that Rowley's method of cultivating his genius was different from Pope's. He certainly had not profited from Pope's advice in the *Essay on Criticism*:

> 'Tis more to *guide* than *spur* the Muse's Steed;
> Restrain his Fury, than provoke his Speed;
> The wingéd Courser, like a gen'rous Horse,
> Shows most true Mettle when you *check* his Course.[5]

The wingéd courser recurs in the verses to William Canynge which Rowley places at the beginning of *Aella*. Rowley is reproving his contemporaries' interest in history rather than poetry, but he also seems to parody the Popean maxim of restraint:

> Cannynge and I from common course dyssente;
> Wee ryde the stede, botte yev to hym the reene;
> Ne wylle betweene crased [broken, old] molterynge bookes be pente,
> Botte soare on hyghe, and yn the sonne-bemes sheene.
>
> (ll. 81–84; *Works*, I, 177–78)[6]

Like many others of his time, Chatterton is impatient with any theory of literature that is not based on the unfettered power of genius.
In his *Conjectures on Original Composition*, Young had written:

With regard to the Moral world, *Conscience*, with regard to the Intellectual, *Genius*, is that God within. Genius can set us right in Composition, without the Rules of the Learned; as Conscience sets us right in Life, without the Laws of the Land: *This*, singly, can make us Good, as Men; *That*, singly as Writers, can, sometimes, make us Great.[7]

Young's statement reminds us that the eighteenth century often viewed the theory of art and the theory of morals as two congruent parts of a larger theory of human nature. The same psychological analysis that could discover an innate capacity for knowing the truth in morals could also discover an innate capacity for creating the beautiful in art. As we might expect, Chatterton believes in conscience as much as he believes in genius. The hero of his modern tale "The Unfortunate Fathers" justifies his suicide by declaring:

There is a principle in man, (a shadow of the divinity) which constitutes him the image of God; you may call it conscience, grace, inspiration, the spirit, or whatever name your education gives it. If a man acts according to this regulator, he is right: if contrary to it, he is wrong. It is an approved truth, that this principle varies in every rational being. As I can reconcile suicide to this principle, with me it is consequently no crime. (*Works*, I, 445)

This is a violent appeal to conscience indeed. Perhaps to allay his readers' suspicions, Chatterton adds that "this seeming philosophy was lost on" his hero's father. Yet as Meyerstein suggests, the philosophy does seem to be Chatterton's.[8] The father is the villain of the piece and cannot be expected to understand, and elsewhere Chatterton implies that the self is, for better or worse, the author of its own standards.[9] One recalls that Chatterton himself, at least according to the traditional account, "dissented" from the "common course" by committing suicide.[10]

But neither Young's statements nor Chatterton's can be taken strictly at face value. Neither Young nor any other British theorist of Chatterton's time consistently maintained that genius or conscience can make a man "Good" or "Great" if it does not enable him to conform in some way to social expectations. Young assumes that conscience and "the Laws of the Land" tell us the same thing, and that an original genius is likely to receive high honor from other men: "An *Original* enters early upon Reputation: *Fame*, fond of new Glories, sounds her Trumpet in Triumph at its birth."[11] Despite his apparent belief that values are merely relative to each person's innate "principle," Chatterton was anxious to provide Rowley, the symbol of his own original genius, with a context of significance founded on social approbation. It was not enough to make the works of his persona ancient, and therefore more interesting to a certain class of readers than his own acknowledged works could possibly have been. He must also provide the ancient original genius with an original audience that would appreciate him; he must surround his persona with a community responsive to his gifts. In this community, Rowley fills the honorable offices of "Biographer, Historiographer, and Poet"; John Lydgate recognizes him as a worthy successor of Chaucer ("John Ladgates Answer," *Works*, I, 62–63); he is the client and confidant of the most powerful member of his society, William Canynge. Canynge's approbation is of the greatest value, since he is the embodiment of all social virtues: "the Mecenas of his time: one who could happily blend The Poet, the Painter, the Priest, and the Christian — perfect in each: a Friend to all in distress, an honor to Bristol, and a Glory to the Church" (*Ryse of Peyncteynge, Works*, I, 259).

Rowley's world is fantastically, even obsessively, detailed. But I think that Frances Schouler Miller is mistaken in suggesting that it is, in a general sense, historically realistic.[12] Rowley and Canynge are significant by the standards of Chatterton's world — not necessarily by those of the fifteenth century. When Rowley and Canynge, judging a case of heresy, declare that they "approve not of invalidating Arguments by violence and Death provided a Man enjoys his Opinion alone," one realizes that Chatterton will allow his heroes to do or say nothing that would forfeit their claim to the virtues approved in his own century (*Nine Deeds and Proclamations, Works*, I, 133). I am not objecting to Chatterton's use of anachronism. It is, of course, a conscious use; in order to create the Rowleyan milieu, he had read enough history to know that toleration of people's private religious sentiments was not a virtue particularly prized by the fifteenth century. I am insisting, however, on Chatterton's desire to give Canynge and Rowley significance as exemplars of the sentimental virtues. The letters, poems, and memoirs of the Rowley circle can be seen as fragments of a sentimental (and a truly bourgeois) romance. The romance is set during the Wars of the Roses, and Chatterton might have chosen warriors as his heroes. Instead, he chooses to exalt the acts of generosity of a merchant's son, the antiquarian researches of a good-hearted priest, the bonds of sentiment between two friends. Walpole had turned the antiquarian romance toward terror; Chatterton turns it toward something that resembles the sentimental novel or drama, in which the sympathies of the audience are awakened by characters made to resemble the audience in its most tender and virtuous moods.

This is one way that Chatterton found to give Rowley the social significance he lacked in his own life. But what of Rowley's significance as an original genius? And what of Rowley's, and Chatterton's, significance as poets of the sublime? Here he might have followed the example of James Macpherson.[13] Macpherson's Ossian combines in one person the warrior and the man of sensibility, the bard of sublime terror and the sentimental poet. Ossian's hero Fingal carries sentimentalism to new heights, even on the battlefield. In *Carric-Thura*, for example, after vanquishing an enemy, Fingal turns to him and his mistress with the most ostentatious compassion:

Fingal pitied the white-armed maid: he stayed the uplifted sword. The tear was in the eye of the king, as, bending forward, he spoke. King of streamy Sora! fear not the sword of Fingal. It was never stained with the blood of the vanquished; it never pierced a fallen foe. Let thy people rejoice along the blue waters of Tora: let the maids of thy love be glad.[14]

On the assumption that human nature has always had the same capacity for moral feeling, Ossian's defenders could see no reason why the poetry of a barbarous age should not be always on the stretch between gothic sublimity and mild sentiment. Hugh Blair wrote:

Some of the qualities indeed which distinguish a Fingal, moderation, humanity, and clemency, would not probably be the first ideas of heroism occurring to a barbarous people: But no sooner had such ideas begun to dawn on the minds of poets, than, as the human mind easily opens to the native representations of human perfection, they would be seized and embraced; they would enter into their panegyricks.[15]

In fact, the time in which Ossian lived was quite the most propitious for the development of genius: "The manners of Ossian's age . . . were abundantly favourable to a poetical genius. The two dispiriting vices, to which Longinus imputes the decline of poetry, covetousness and effeminacy, were as yet unknown."[16]

Chatterton might have found these comments appended to the

edition in which he read Ossian's poetry. He could have used them as a formula for creating his own persona. Macpherson's success undoubtedly helped inspire him to concoct his own antique poetry. But although he directly imitated Ossian in a number of gothic "translations," he seems to have known that Ossian's sentiments did not ring true. He parodied them in "Memoirs of a Sad Dog": "Behold! thou art happy; but soon, ah! soon, wilt thou be miserable. Thou art as easy and tranquil as the face of the green-mantled puddle; but soon, ah! soon, wilt thou be tumbled and tossed by misfortunes, like the stream of the water-mill" (*Works,* I, 654).[17] It is certain that an Ossianic hero could never express Chatterton's unique identity. What relation could such a hero bear to a young boy of antiquarian interests struggling for a literary career in a commercial town? In order to write his epics, after all, Macpherson had been forced to submerge his own identity completely — not just to evade detection, but also to embody a pure and ancient form of human nature in both his heroes and his bard.[18]

Chatterton's difficulty, then, was in discovering how to give his persona significance without destroying its usefulness as a projection of his own distinct identity. Part of the solution was to make Rowley an inhabitant of his own town, in modest circumstances, like himself, and eager in pursuing his own antiquarian interests. But Rowley's poetic excellence, though great, was not sufficient to give him the significance that Chatterton required for his persona; Rowley's excellence as a man and as a poet must be recognized by society. Here William Canynge, the great fifteenth-century magnate, was doubly useful: he provided Rowley with the sympathy he deserved, and he provided Chatterton with yet another surrogate identity. It is impossible not to recognize Chatterton's likeness in the precocious Canynge, who "eate downe Learneynge wyth the Wastle Cake" and who was despised by the avaricious because "he bente not hys wholle rede to gette Lukre" (*Rowley's Heraldic Account, Lyfe of W: Canynge, Works,* I, 245, 228–29).[19]

In order to make the situation of Rowley and Canynge correspond in some fashion with his own, Chatterton was forced to make them much more civilized and domestic than Macpherson's heroes.

In order to give them a specific identity that was recognizably his own, Chatterton could adopt only half of the Ossianic formula. Rowley and Canynge could be men of reflection, but not of action; heroes of sensibility but not of sublimity. Again, the problem: how could Chatterton show that both he and Rowley were poets of the highest order, capable of experiencing and expressing the sublime?

One solution might be to make Rowley the "translator" of works written in a truly primitive age, an age in which no sentimental virtues restrained men from feeling the full sublimity of heroic action. This is what Chatterton does in two of his earlier works, the two successive versions of *The Battle of Hastings*. Rowley supposedly based these poems on a work by the eleventh-century monk Turgot, and they have all the gothic sublimity of Ossian, but without the sentiment. Ossian, in fact, frequently prefers to describe the emotions of his characters as they prepare for or return from battle, rather than the details of battle itself; Turgot is much more interested in "Deathdoeynge Blades," battle lines foaming like waves, and arrows falling like stars (I.50, 121–30, II.234–36; *Works*, I, 28, 30, 75). Chatterton's editor Donald S. Taylor likens *Battle of Hastings I* to "billiards — A kills B; in revenge C kills A; in revenge D kills C; and so on" (*Works*, II, 823). Chatterton is, perhaps, a little more interested in developing characters in his second version of the *Battle*, but he never grows particularly sentimental about them: "His eyne shotte fyre, lyke blazyng starre at nyghte, / He grypd his swerde, and felle upon the place of fyghte" (II.309–10; *Works*, I, 77).

Such heroes are icons that the primitive Turgot usually worships naively. And the ability to evoke their spirit seems to make Chatterton himself feel of some consequence as a bard. About one of them he asks: "What blazours then, what glorie shall he clayme, / What doughtie Homere shall hys praises synge?" (II.441–42; *Works*, I, 80). Chatterton himself, of course, is the "doughtie Homere," the original genius fit to sing heroic deeds. He is capable of a certain amount of irony at the expense of his characters, especially if they are Norman enemies. He likens one of them to a "Mountein Oke" that

> viewe[d] the Briars below with selftaught Pride —
> But whan thrown down by mightie Thunder stroke,
> Hede rather be a Bryer than a Oke.   (I.155–60; *Works*, I, 31)

The naive gothicism of the *Battle* prevents Chatterton, however, from exploring the psychological origins of his pasteboard characters' "selftaught Pride."

A short time later, Chatterton wrote his drama *Aella*, and here he chose a poetic vehicle that allowed him to give the hero of sublime action a psychological dimension. Although *Aella* is set in Saxon times, it is the creation not of some naive, monkish chronicler, but of the relatively sophisticated Rowley, who has somewhat advanced notions about what a "tragedie" should be. In his prefatory verses, Rowley refuses to be chained to fact: poetry may "sometymes soare 'bove trouthe of hystorie." It should not be written with a "keppened" — a cautious — pen: "Vearse maie be goode, botte poesie wantes more, / An onlist [boundless] lecturn [subject], and a songe adygne [praiseworthy]." Rowley finds his "boundless subject" in the warrior Aella; he will write "somme great storie of a manne" (ll. 88–94, 44; *Works*, I, 178, 176). Chatterton is willing to suspend his historical sense of what the primitive hero actually was in order to give Rowley the freedom to present him in his own way and to consider him according to his own, more modern standards.

But the result is a hero whose personal significance is very difficult to measure. By suspending his historical sense, Chatterton is able to follow the Ossianic formula and present Aella both as the sentimental lover for whom "On [one] smyle woulde be suffycyll mede" and as the warrior for whom battle is something sublime:

> Lyche a rodde [red] gronfer [meteor], shalle mie anlace sheene,
> Lyche a strynge lyoncelle I'lle bee ynne fyghte,
> Lyche fallynge leaves the Dacyannes [Danes] shalle bee sleene,
> Lyche a loud dynnynge streeme scalle be mie myghte.
> Ye menne, who woulde deserve the name of knyghte,
> Lette bloddie teares bie all your paves [shields] be wepte.
>   (ll. 180, 760–65; *Works*, I, 181, 203)

In all this, Rowley is sympathetic with his hero; Aella is clearly a "boundless subject" because he has a boundless soul, one that unites

the sublime and the sentimental. He is significant, just as many of
Macpherson's heroes are, both as a lover and as a representative of
the heroic virtue honored by his society. Yet the Ossianic formula
finally does not work. Aella is not a complete hero because he is not
a complete self. He lives in fear of losing his identity — an identity
that he generally bases on his social significance, his "honnoure" as a
warrior and leader of men.[20] As a result, the two halves of Aella's
self can never be integrated into a whole person.

Aella's crisis of identity begins when he is called to leave his bride
in order to lead his men against invading Danes. Birtha begs him to
stay, but a subordinate's appeal convinces him that he can only affirm his identity by fulfilling his social duty. "Mie soulghe dothe
nowe begynne to see herselle," he says:

> Yette I wylle bee mieselfe, and rouze mie spryte
> To acte wythe rennome, and goe meet the bloddie fyghte.
>
> (ll. 397, 404–05; *Works*, I, 190)

There is some question in Aella's mind about whether his identity
ought instead to be based on his love for Birtha — "I'm flyynge from
mieselfe yn flying thee" — but he represses it (l. 503; *Works*, I, 194).
When he returns from routing the Danes, he discovers Birtha gone,
erroneously suspects her of infidelity, and slays himself. His motive
is not so much loss of love as loss of honor, and the loss of identity
this implies: "I once was Aella; nowe bee notte yttes shade" (l. 1302;
Works, I, 224).

Chatterton has depicted the divided self, but his analysis never
culminates in any statement of values about it. The play ends with a
speech that seems to criticize Aella's devotion to honor — "Aella, thie
rennome was thie onlie gayne; / For yatte, thie pleasaunce, and thie
joie was loste" — but that actually awards him the honor he sought:
"A just amede [reward] to thee to bee, / Inne heaven thou synge of
Godde, on erthe we'lle synge of thee" (ll. 1360–65; *Works*, I, 228).
One remembers that it is the villain Celmonde who has previously
criticized the notion of honor: "Honnoure, whatt bee ytte? tys a
shadowes shade, / A thynge of wychencref, an idle dreme" (ll. 536–
37; *Works*, I, 195). Chatterton never establishes the proper basis of
identity; the issue is never resolved. Irvin B. Kroese has attributed

this flaw in *Aella* to a flaw in Chatterton's own psychology: Aella's addiction to honor is a reflection of Chatterton's own "pride," which Kroese calls his "pseudo-self."[21] Certainly, Chatterton found his pride a "distracting," and yet an "unconquerable" part of his identity. Yet I think that there was also something else that prevented him from resolving the problem of identity and personal significance in *Aella*.

To some extent, Chatterton's persona was out of his control. His "pseudo-self" was, in fact, Rowley. Rowley represented the way he wanted to be seen by the world; Rowley was a poet endowed with all the literary and social significance that Chatterton himself wished to achieve. Chatterton constructed his identity as Rowley, not just from the characteristics of his own personality, but also from his conception of what society thought an original genius should be. He could have derived this conception most easily from Ossian and from contemporary works on original genius. Duff's *Essay on Original Genius* provides a good example of the type of thinking responsible for Rowley. Duff describes the genius capable of creating an epic as one characterized by "an extreme sensibility," one that "will admirably succeed in the invention of pathetic as well as sublime sentiments." In tragedy, genius usually manifests itself by making "virtue . . . appear great and venerable in distress"; the epic must, and tragedy should, exhibit characters who are both "virtuous and illustrious," "complete models of excellence" who combine all the "shining qualities which constitute the Hero."[22] These are broad and heavy strokes; in tone and emphasis, if in nothing else, such comments are far removed from Aristotle. In *Aella*, Chatterton is at pains to make Rowley a poet of sensibility and Aella a "complete model" of sentimental "excellence." He falls, awkwardly enough, into the Ossianic mode. Aella is as sympathetic in peace, when he comforts his erstwhile enemies with bread and wine, as he is sublime in battle (ll. 1214–23; *Works*, I, 220–21). Rowley's significance as a poet — and as a surrogate identity for Chatterton — is derived, in part, from Aella's significance as a hero: both must represent the highest ideals. In order for *Aella* to be a tragedy, of course, its hero must be shown "in distress"; and his quest for honor is useful in providing a suitable pretext for his tragic death. Chatterton himself is clearly interested in analyzing the question of whether one should base his self-esteem, or his identity, on "pride" or "honor." But Rowley cannot be expected to analyze Aella's crisis of identity very deeply; in doing so, he might be forced to criticize his own sensibility, his own genius, the values he himself holds and embodies in his hero.

This distinction between Chatterton and Rowley may seem forced, but it is apparent that Chatterton's self-expression was channeled and limited in many ways by his persona. For example: One of the most salient characteristics of Chatterton's works in modern English is a vein of abusive satire that is obviously an expression of one aspect of his identity. But as Miller points out, Rowley does not indulge himself in this way.[23] As an original genius of the highest order, he possesses a more delicate sensibility. Another example: Chatterton was deeply frustrated by the conditions of his birth and upbringing, and continually aspired to a higher social position as a poet or antiquarian. Yet in *Eclogue the Third*, he permits Rowley to write a lengthy sermon on the folly of desiring to better oneself socially.

Examples might be multiplied: to *be* Rowley, Chatterton had to *think* as Rowley would have. Whether Rowley was conceived as essentially a man of the eighteenth or of the fifteenth century, conflicts were bound to arise between him and Chatterton. But Chatterton was capable, to a remarkable degree, of entering into the perceptions of his persona. In the *Bristowe Tragedie*, for instance, Rowley describes the execution of an heroic knight by the evil King Edward, and he concludes with these words:

> Thus was the ende of Bawdin's fate:
> Godde prosper longe oure kynge,
> And grante hee maye, wyth Bawdin's soule,
> Ynne heav'n Godd's mercie synge!
>
> (ll. 389–92; *Works*, I, 20)

Nothing could better evoke Rowley's sympathy for Baldwin and his simultaneous reluctance to criticize the king to whom he is subject. It is amusing to find one of the defenders of the authenticity of the Rowley poems, Walter Whiter, arguing on the basis of associationist principles that artistic "spirit and animation," such as we see in the splendid scene painting of *Eclogue the Second*, "can never be created by the abstract workings of the mind; but are the immediate and necessary productions of an external agency" — that is, of experience.[24] On the contrary: Chatterton's effects are the result of a much more complex process, his imaginative sympathy with the "experience" of Rowley, his own creation. This is the power of vision that Blake might possibly have been thinking of when he owned himself an admirer of both Rowley and Chatterton.[25] It is a power that is no less remarkable than Chatterton's command of images and his facility in the Rowleyan tongue.

But as I have tried to show, Chatterton's difficulties in handling his persona were many. And they cannot be attributed entirely to his youth. Surely we may expect more from a skillful and industrious prodigy than we may from an ordinary adolescent, and Chatterton often fulfills our expectations admirably. He was, perhaps, the truest "original genius" in literature that eighteenth-century Britain ever produced, and Rowley was in many ways the truest expression of his identity. But Rowley was not intended merely as an expression of identity; he was also intended as an expression of Chatterton's ideal significance as a creative self. Chatterton had Rowley proclaim that "Cannynge and I from common course dyssente," but Chatterton could not simply evolve his own standards for judging the significance of his persona. Rowley must be justified by his conformity to those conceptions of the creative self that Chatterton found in the literature and aesthetics of his time. Rowley's virtues — his eager sensibility, his moral idealism — and his deficiencies — his frequent shallowness, his sentimentality — show something of the virtues and deficiencies of those conceptions.

CHAPTER SEVEN

Self and Perception:
William Cowper

In the *Defence of Poetry*, Shelley refers to literature as a teacher of "self-knowledge and self-respect" and observes that "neither the eye nor the mind can see itself, unless reflected upon that which it re-sembles."[1] This concept of self-knowledge would not have surprised Shelley's eighteenth-century predecessors. The idea that the self can discover its nature and significance by sympathetic identification with something in the outside world is fundamental to many eighteenth-century theories of psychology and literature. Some of the most interesting expressions of this concept can be found in the poetry of William Cowper. Not only does Cowper laud sympathy as a moral force in a number of his poems,[2] but he fills his writings with images based on his sympathetic identifications—with the stricken deer, the Yardley Oak, the Castaway, and even the God whom he wished, in his own way, to "resemble." As one of his recent critics, William Norris Free, has remarked, Cowper "had to seek subjects external to himself with which he would feel a kindred spirit" because he could not "confront his deepest feelings in a more direct manner."[3] It is not that Cowper avoided introspection; in his poetry and letters he is constantly meditating upon himself. But his chronic mental illness made it difficult for him to trust his own per-ceptions, and he turned to nature and the Bible to find a standard of truth and a source of images in which he could recognize accurate reflections of his own elusive self.

When Edward Young referred to the self as the "Stranger within thee," he was exhorting his readers to discover themselves by look-ing more deeply into their own minds. But the ability to gain an accurate view of the self, as well as of the rest of the world, also requires the ability to escape somehow from the self and its subjective impressions. Despite all his efforts, this was what Cowper was ultimately unable to do, and his failure is usually imputed to his mental disorder. At this late date, it is difficult to diagnose his condition with confidence; it may have been what one modern psychiatrist pronounced it — a "manic-depressive psychosis."[4] Yet as most of his readers have probably discovered to their surprise, the really virulent forms of Cowper's psychosis exerted a remarkably small effect on his works. No one is a more genial companion than Cowper in most of his letters and longer poems, and this might perhaps lead one to question whether he was severely unbalanced, or even decidedly unhappy, during most of his poetic career. Cowper's own description of his character is likely the most judicious: "My mind has always a melancholy cast, and is like some pools I have seen, which, though filled with a black and putrid water, will nevertheless, in a bright day, reflect the sunbeams from the surface."[5] And, according to his own testimony, Cowper did not find melancholy altogether "unpleasing" nor "without its use."[6]

But it is questionable whether the method that Cowper habitually chose for attaining objectivity — finding external images with which to identify himself and external standards with which to evaluate his significance — could really have helped him to see himself much more clearly than he could by introspection alone. Even if a person believes that he has found an objective standard of judgment, a standard such as Cowper found in his religion, he must still rely on his own perceptions to interpret that standard and apply it to himself. Furthermore, if one has already formed a conception of what one is, one may not be able to identify oneself with any image that does not correspond to that conception, however delusive one's idea of oneself may actually be.

What I have said so far of the process of sympathetic identification advocated in eighteenth-century literature and psychological theory indicates that this process, as a means of knowledge, may have highly ambiguous results. As Dr. Johnson's friend Elizabeth Carter observes, one may well find images in the external world that one considers "expressive" of one's "own inconstant Self": the world provides a mirror in which reflections of the self may be seen.[7] But is not the self also a mirror? One need not be a philosopher to remark the fact that the mind which seeks its reflection in the external world is itself, to a great degree, a "reflection" of its past experience of that world — and further, that the self, as "mirror," casts reflections of its own established modes of thought upon its observations of the world. Eighteenth-century and Romantic references to "mirror" effects in mental processes often tempt one to imagine mind and world as paired mirrors in which images of the self appear in infinite regress: the images are endlessly insistent, but it is hard to determine just where — in which of the two opposing glasses — the procession of diminishing forms began. All of this has much to do with William Cowper's difficulties as a man and as a poet. Distrustful of his own abnormally delicate sensibility, he sought external images that could provide defining reflections of himself. Yet he could not firmly distinguish the objective from the subjective, a true reflection from a delusive image of the self projected by his own mind.

Cowper's difficulty in escaping from his subjective impressions was increased by the fact that he had two powerful reasons for placing some degree of faith in his immediate, subjective experience — reasons that proceeded from the theological and aesthetic assumptions of his time. The first had to do with the nature of his evangelical religion. Although Cowper's neo-Calvinism was based primarily on revealed truth, it also appealed to the testimony of individual experience. The Reverend John Newton, Cowper's spiritual mentor, wrote these remarks as a preface to the volume of poems that Cowper published in 1782:

At a time when hypothesis and conjecture in philosophy are so justly exploded, and little is considered as deserving the name of knowledge, which will not stand the test of experiment, the very use of the term *experimental*, in religious concernments, is by too many unhappily rejected with disgust. But we well know, that they who affect to despise the inward feelings which religious persons speak of, and to treat them as enthusiasm and folly, have inward feelings of their own, which, though they would, they cannot suppress.[8]

Cowper's "experimental" version of Protestantism encouraged him to base his poetry on an empirical view of his own feelings.

Second, Cowper was forced to rely on his individual perception by his poetic needs and goals. As a disciple of the eighteenth-century faith in originality, he wished to express experience that was completely his own. "My descriptions," he writes in a letter to the Reverend William Unwin, "are all from nature: not one of them second-handed. My delineations of the heart are from my own experience: not one of them borrowed from books, or in the least degree conjectural."[9] Cowper intends his poetry to teach religious doctrine, but he also intends it to possess the immediacy of personal observation.

But how was objective truth — for Cowper, revealed truth — to be reconciled with spontaneous experience? Cowper could never really decide that question. Sometimes he appears to exalt the self's perceptive power as a source of truth, comparing the poet's eye to the sun, which "shed[s] illuminating rays / On ev'ry scene and subject it surveys," or declaring that "Truths, that the theorist could never reach, / And observation taught me, I would teach."[10] In *The Task*, he states that a poet's goal is

> T' arrest the fleeting images that fill
> The mirror of the mind, and hold them fast,
> And force them sit till he has pencil'd off
> A faithful likeness of the forms he views.   (II.290–93)

Yet this commonsense mimetic theory (which, by the way, seems rather inconsistent with Cowper's image of the poetic eye as something that adds rather than merely reflects light) is very difficult to maintain for anyone who realizes that his perceptions depend on his mental attitude as well as on what his eye literally sees. In "The Shrubbery," Cowper shows that he is quite conscious of this:

> Me fruitful scenes and prospects waste
>   Alike admonish not to roam;
> These tell me of enjoyments past,
>   And those of sorrows yet to come.   (ll. 21–24)

In the process of perception, the world may mirror the self as much as the self mirrors the world.

To use Cowper's own imagery, perception is like "colour'd crystal" that changes the appearance of the objects seen through it: "Thus things terrestrial wear a diff'rent hue, / As youth or age persuades; and neither true" (*Hope*, ll. 69–74). But this metaphor of colored glass does not express the full complexity of the problem of perception as Cowper understood it. The image implies that people see things in the way in which they are conditioned to see them, but it does not express the additional difficulty that they see things in the way in which they *desire* to see them. Faulty perception allows people to impose upon reality the images that they need to see. At the beginning of *Truth*, Cowper finds a metaphor for this:

> Man, on the dubious waves of error toss'd,
> His ship half founder'd, and his compass lost,
> Sees, far as human optics may command,
> A sleeping fog, and fancies it dry land:
> Spreads all his canvass, ev'ry sinew plies;
> Pants for't, aims at it, enters it, and dies! (ll. 1–6)

The act of perception, then, may also be an unconscious but willful act of interpretation.

As I will show, Cowper himself was often unable to tell where perception stops and interpretation begins. In fact, the image of a man seeking salvation with only his own "optics" to guide him might be taken as an excellent image of its author. Nevertheless, Cowper was consciously concerned with the danger of moral relativism, and he knew it as a danger that arises when people become so conscious of the self's individual way of viewing the world that they cease to believe that it is possible to discover truth. That is why, in *Hope*, he satirizes the fashionable speech of the churchman Smug, who observes that

> Fallible man . . .
> Is still found fallible, however wise;
> And diff'ring judgments serve but to declare
> That truth lies somewhere, if we knew but where. (ll. 421–24)

In *Retirement*, however, Cowper asserts that the problem is not just our consciousness of the uncertainty of our perceptions, but also our failure to direct and "limit" them:

> 'tis not easy with a mind like our's,
> Conscious of weakness in its noblest pow'rs,
> And in a world where, other ills apart,
> The roving eye misleads the careless heart,
> To limit thought, by nature prone to stray
> Wherever freakish fancy points the way.   (ll. 123–28)

The idea that the "fancy" should not direct one's thoughts is, of course, an eighteenth-century commonplace. Even the sentimental novelist Mackenzie, who is normally an advocate of indulging one's sensibility, is anxious for young people not "to forget, amidst the intricacies of sentiment, or the dreams of sensibility, the truths of reason, or the laws of principle."[11] It therefore comes as no surprise when Cowper insists that his readers should let revealed religion guide their perceptions, particularly their perceptions of themselves. He urges them to "dive into the secret deeps within," but only to "measure all that passes in the breast" by the laws of God. One is not to be preoccupied with simply trying to understand one's personality; the proper goal of introspection is knowledge not only about "ourselves" but also about "our recov'ry from our fall" (*Retirement*, ll. 129–38). Cowper has an unusually strict religious concern, but like many other writers of his period he is interested less in determining the self's identity than in determining its moral significance; and he insists that personal value can only be measured by looking to a standard external to the self. In *The Task*, Cowper can declare that the person who "attends to his interior self" has "no unimportant, though a silent, task" (III.373–78). In *Charity*, however, he shows that he associates an inward-turning examination of the self with an outward-turning contemplation of God:

> Self-knowledge, truly learn'd, of course implies
> The rich possession of a nobler prize;
> For self to self, and God to man, reveal'd,
> (Two themes to nature's eye for ever seal'd)

Are taught by rays that fly with equal pace
From the same centre of enlight'ning grace.   (ll. 359–64)

The goal is not just to know God; it is also to identify oneself with one's "author, guardian, friend" so that the soul may take "the resemblance of the good she views" (ll. 395–403). Interestingly, Cowper finds in this process, which may be called a type of sympathetic identification, the basis of the self's sympathy with other human beings (ll. 404–34).

Nevertheless, Cowper's basic assumption still seems to be that the only adequate perception is a carefully controlled and "limited" one. Stated in this way, the idea seems paradoxical.[12] But Cowper insists upon it even when he is discussing the self's perception of God's activity in nature. After allowing his "glance of fancy" to survey a variety of natural wonders, he faints before his own vision of the Creator's power:

Absorb'd in that immensity I see,
I shrink abas'd, and yet aspire to thee;
Instruct me, guide me, to that heav'nly day
Thy words more clearly than thy works display,
That, while thy truths my grosser thoughts refine,
I may resemble thee and call thee mine.

                                    (*Retirement*, ll. 93–98)

Cowper wishes to turn from his spontaneous awareness of God's "works" to a more specific study of God's "words"; in effect, he desires to narrow his perceptions so that he can focus on what he can be sure is most clearly true.

The lines I have just quoted are hardly the finest example of Cowper's devotional poetry. His tone is almost theatrical, his diction little more than a set of clichés. But in this instance Cowper's thought is more interesting than the words he finds to express it. Ironically, one of his reasons for desiring to remake himself in God's image is the need to keep the self inviolate. As I have noted in a previous chapter, one of the standard concepts of eighteenth-century aesthetics was the notion that the self naturally becomes assimilated to – in Cowper's words, "absorb'd in" – sublime objects. It was usually assumed (naively enough, as it may appear to us) that this process demonstrates and enhances the self's significance. But writers of a mystical bent, such as Cowper and Blake, were able to recognize the negative implications of sympathetic identification with one's spontaneous perceptions of nature. The danger was that the sublime, however inspiring it might initially seem, could devour personality. The self might become passive or "abas'd," unable to find any stable principle with which to identify. It was because he needed to discover some personal reference in an apparently impersonal universe that Cowper believed in directing and limiting his perceptions.

In a letter written to John Newton in 1780, Cowper discusses his belief that man's consciousness is of no significance if it consists merely of perceptions of a material world. To a point, at least, he is delighted to assimilate himself to nature: "O! I could spend whole days and moonlight nights in feeding upon a lovely prospect! My eyes drink the rivers as they flow." But the self's real support is not its perception of nature, but its knowledge of its own relationship to something higher than nature:

I delight in baubles, and know them to be so; for rested in, and viewed without a reference to their Author, what is the earth—what are the planets—what is the sun itself but a bauble? Better for a man never to have seen them, or to see them with the eyes of a brute, stupid and unconscious of what he beholds, than not to be able to say, 'The Maker of all these wonders is my friend!'"[13]

The only image of himself with which Cowper could rest content, that of a friend of God, could not be found by means of spontaneous perceptions; it could be discovered only in the realm of transcendental ideas.

But one's immediate perceptions are necessarily part of oneself, and Cowper was proud of the fact that his poetry was based on his own direct observations. In his writing, therefore, he wished to allow freedom to his perceptions, but he also wished to impose upon them the forms of his moral and religious beliefs. It is notorious that many of Cowper's poems, especially *The Task*, do not appear to contain a unified progression of ideas and images. In some cases, this problem results, not just from lack of discipline or an imperfect imitation of the Horatian manner, but also from a restless wandering from one mode of observation to another. Cowper alternately attempts to observe the world empirically and to interpret it morally and theologically, often without developing the full potential of either mode.

A striking example of this is the meditation on natural scenery with which Cowper opens Book VI of *The Task*. His general organization of images is associational: the sound of distant bells awakens a "sympathy" in Cowper's heart and reminds him of past scenes in which he has had similar experiences. With "all the cells / Where mem'ry slept" opened by the music of the bells, Cowper remembers his youth and reflects on his thoughtlessness toward his father (ll. 1–43). Part of this passage might be cited as a classic example of empirical psychology generating poetic images. Cowper describes an essentially passive sensibility directed by external stimuli. But it is not long before he drifts into another form of imagery, and the natural world changes from the object of direct perception to the source of a highly conventional moral symbolism. Cowper represents the difficult course of life as a "rugged path, / And prospect oft so dreary and forlorn" and as a veritable "vale of tears"; he likens his father's face to

> the clouds of spring, [which] might low'r,
> And utter now and then an awful voice,
> But had a blessing in its darkest frown,
> Threat'ning at once and nourishing the plant.
>
> (ll. 20–21, 48, 33–36)

Cowper quickly enters a realm of biblical symbolism reminiscent of his Olney Hymns: instead of a literal landscape, he now contemplates a "world" that is a moral "wilderness" (ll. 50–56). Cowper has ceased to explore the details of his private experience — what he sees or hears, what exactly he remembers. Here, as in his spiritual autobiography, the personal experience that determines identity acquires structure and significance as it is viewed in moral and religious terms. It is almost as if Cowper's experience would have no meaning, or could not be examined, if it could not be identified with symbols bearing obvious moral meanings.[14]

Yet very soon Cowper insists that one's immediate perceptions are the key to truth. After surveying the natural landscape in some detail, he asserts that

> Here the heart
> May give an useful lesson to the head,
> And learning wiser grow without his books.
>
> . . . .
>
> Knowledge dwells
> In heads replete with thoughts of other men;
> Wisdom in minds attentive to their own.   (ll. 85–91)

Cowper contrasts secondhand learning with the truth directly perceptible in nature, for she

> Deceive[s] no student. Wisdom there, and truth,
> Not shy, as in the world, and to be won
> By slow solicitation, seize at once
> The roving thought, and fix it on themselves.   (ll. 114–17)

These lines are analogous to the passage in *Retirement* in which Cowper argues that truth can only be known if one "limits" one's perception; but here it is a truth embodied in nature, not God's Word, that — almost like a living creature — "seizes" the mind and properly "fixes" it. Cowper is close to expressing complete faith in empirical observation.

But what is the truth that is to be won by the self's response to nature? It is the knowledge that "there lives and works / A soul in all things, and that soul is God" (ll. 184–85). Cowper sees the cycle of nature as a "miracle" comparable to the sun's arrested motion above the field of Gibeon (ll. 118–33). These truths, of course, do not come directly from Cowper's spontaneous observations of trees and lanes, as he implies. In this instance, at least, he approaches them only by selecting and manipulating natural images so that they correspond with his preexisting beliefs.[15] Cowper's way of thinking — or at least of constructing poetry — is sometimes close to being solipsistic. By this I hardly mean to imply that a reliance on religious faith is in itself solipsistic; the character of Cowper's beliefs is not in question, but rather his method of forming and expressing them. Often, when Cowper imagines he is taking a fresh look at the outside world, he is actually, in his unconsciously revealing phrase, attentive mainly to his own thoughts.

As Free has said, *The Task* is the product of Cowper's desire "to follow the moment-to-moment, day-to-day ramblings" of his own mind, to express the self that he constantly experiences: his interests, his opinions, his habits of perception, and his way of life.[16] The poem includes, as part of this elaborate view of the self and its occupations, many original and detailed observations of nature and moving statements of religious faith. Still, one is justified in giving serious attention to the perceptual basis of Cowper's poetry. He himself was concerned about the danger of being trapped within his own subjective perceptions, yet this fear seems only to have exacerbated his problem: it made him wish to believe that no matter how idiosyncratic his perceptions might be, they could somehow be verified objectively.

This is especially true of his perceptions of himself. After forming an evaluation of himself in his own mind, he sought to give it authority by finding in the external world a correlative image for his condition — often a conventional image sanctioned by religious precedent. Cowper's references to himself as a solitary wanderer in a moral "wilderness" or as a stricken deer singled out for divine aid are examples of this practice;[17] and surely it seems a harmless one, until one realizes, from Cowper's habitual use of some very similar images, that he is almost unable to see himself except through the medium of a rather limited and somewhat arbitrary set of symbols.[18] For Cowper, such images, habitually indulged, became more than an expression of one aspect of experience; they became almost a method of thinking, a way of viewing the self objectively. A letter written to Newton in 1784 shows the direction in which Cowper's mind typically moved:

The weather is an exact emblem of my mind in its present state. A thick fog envelopes every thing, and at the same time it freezes intensely. You will tell me that this cold gloom will be succeeded by a cheerful spring, and endeavour to encourage me to hope for a spiritual change resembling it; —but it will be lost labour. Nature revives again; but a soul once slain lives no more. The hedge that has been apparently dead, is not so; it will burst into leaf and blossom at the appointed time; but no such time is appointed for the stake that stands in it. It is as dead as it seems, and will prove itself no dissembler.[19]

Although Cowper knows that "a thick fog" envelops his perceptions, he allows no appeal from them. He uses his search for emblems of truth in the external world as a means of validating an opinion of himself that he has already formed, an opinion that he refuses to challenge by interpreting these emblems differently. In his poems and letters he identifies himself with a storm-tossed ship, a solitary pillar of crumbling rock, a shattered and equally solitary tree—a host of determinedly negative images.[20] The outside world provides him with a mirror of himself, but it is, after all, a mirror distorted by his own ideas.

The best example of this, of course, is Cowper's identification of himself as a castaway. In his early hymns, he sought to examine himself by the infallible standard of God's Word, in which he discovered a number of different emblems of what he potentially might become—not only a "cast-away" or a mariner on a "shatter'd bark," but also a welcome guest at the Lord's table or a thorn blooming like the myrtle.[21] But in later years, the conviction grew on him that he had, in fact, been cast off by God. For this belief there was, as his friends and religious advisors assured him, no objective evidence whatever. But Cowper confused his own agonized appraisal of his sins with the judgment of God. By the time he wrote his final poem, his identification of himself with one purely negative image had become so complete that he regarded his own metaphor as objective, unarguable fact. He was no longer William Cowper, who could be perceived in a variety of different ways; he was, inescapably, his own selected perception—the Castaway.

Morris Golden has suggested that Cowper's poetry is most vital, and most interesting, when he is able to see the world "clearly organized as a picture of . . . himself";[22] "The Castaway" is good evidence that his poetry can gain power and definition from his search for images of himself in the external world. But it is hardly accidental that this poem is the only one of his works that retains even a shadowy popularity. As Golden says, Cowper is an artist "of limited though intense scope," but his limitations are all too evident. Cowper often gives us, not a more profound view, even of himself, but only one more view of what we have come to expect from him. One need not indulge the traditional wish that Cowper had somehow been less domestic, somehow more like Wordsworth, in order to feel this.

We might say of Cowper what Henry Crabb Robinson said of one of his own unfortunate friends: "His malady lay in a diseased endeavour to obey the injunction, 'Nosce teipsum.'"[23] One of the leading characteristics of Cowper's "disease" was a heightened, exaggerated form of that sensibility which was regarded in his own time as a mark of genius. When Cowper was sane enough to place responsibility for his condition on his own psychology rather than divine predestination, he characterized himself as primarily a man of sensibility: "I am not naturally insensible, and the sensibilities that I had by nature have been wonderfully enhanced by a long series of shocks, given to a frame of nerves that was never very athletic. I feel accordingly, whether painful or pleasant, in the extreme."[24] Cowper's friend and biographer William Hayley, viewing Cowper's condition from the outside, also thought in terms of sensibility: Cowper possessed "a frame distinguished by nerves of the most delicate and dangerous sensibility"; and this delicacy, Hayley implies, may have been responsible both for "the happy perfection of his genius" and for "the calamitous eclipses of his effulgent mind."[25] William Hazlitt, a much finer and more perceptive analyst, found little enough to praise in Cowper's delicate sensibility, but he finally forgave his "morbid affection," because "it is the nature of the poetical temperament to carry every thing to excess . . . and to find torment or rapture in that in which others merely find a resource from *ennui*, or a relaxation from common occupation."[26]

"Sensibility" is a term that may cover a multitude of weaknesses — or excellences. But it is surely "sensibility," in a disturbingly pure form, that one sees in Cowper, with all its eighteenth-century associations of extreme sensitivity and intense interest in the way in which the self is affected, or wishes to be affected, by what it perceives. And in Cowper's poetry one sees, in a particularly pure form, some of the problems implicit in sensibility: the problem of deciding what "limits" ought to be placed on the perceiving self, the question of what "feelings" ought to be used in determining the nature of the self and its position in the world, the problem of distinguishing subjective perceptions from objective truth. This last issue naturally becomes of crucial importance to the man, and the poet, of sensibility, who is often likely, if we can believe the poets and aestheticians of the later eighteenth century, to be "overpowered" by his own feelings.

As I have shown, Cowper wished to base his poetry on his "experimental" knowledge of his own feelings; his aesthetic beliefs, and even his religion, encouraged him to do so. His sensibility was of central importance to his art. A "delicate sensibility," such as Cowper had, should presumably give one finer perceptions of the world and of oneself, but one may become so engrossed by one's feelings that one becomes incapable of seeing anything objectively. Although Cowper sought to view himself more clearly by sympathetic identification with other persons and objects, he did not succeed in escaping from his own subjectivity. Sympathy did not function for him as a way of liberating the self; in fact, Cowper's struggles usually succeeded only in emphasizing a fundamental contradiction in the philosophy of sympathy to which many of his contemporaries gave a largely uncritical assent. Perception is really selective and interpretive; and sympathetic perception may become a means, not of learning anything new about oneself or the rest of the world, but only of identifying something in the outside world with one's settled image of oneself. It is this self-oriented, reversed sympathy that produced "The Castaway"; as Cowper says in that poem, "misery still delights to trace / Its 'semblance in another's case" (ll. 59–60).[27] Cowper's writings show that sympathy and sensibility — which should aid the self in gaining new impressions and communicating more freely with the rest of the world — may actually reinforce the self's isolation.

CHAPTER EIGHT

Self as Creative Genius:
William Blake

As a Romantic poet well suited to twentieth-century tastes, William Blake is often studied in isolation from his background in the eighteenth century. But it is idle to imagine that the problems of the self that disturbed the so-called pre-Romantics evaporated with the dawn of Romanticism. Blake had studied the works of his eighteenth-century predecessors in poetry—Young, Gray, Macpherson, Chatterton, Cowper—as their admirer and sometimes as their illustrator. And he had been profoundly affected, often with something less than admiration, by what he knew of the works of his seventeenth- and eighteenth-century predecessors in philosophy. His attempt to solve the problems of personal identity and significance that were posed in these works involved a comprehensive revision, but not necessarily a comprehensive rejection, of earlier solutions.

Blake's philosophy of the self is frequently considered the direct antithesis of eighteenth-century empirical psychology. This view results, perhaps, from a failure clearly to distinguish empiricism from rationalism—a failure that is Blake's as much as his commentators'. He was typically more interested in reproving philosophical error than in making careful distinctions between philosophical schools. The exact nature of his own theory of knowledge is notoriously difficult to determine. He seems to align himself with the empiricists by preferring immediate perception to deductive reasoning: "Knowledge is not by deduction but Immediate by Perception or Sense at once."[1] But because he places imagination above simple, unmediated perception, his attitude toward "Perception or Sense" is complex indeed. Around 1789 he scratched in the margin of Emanuel Swedenborg's *Divine Love* a denunciation of "worldly wisdom or demonstration by the senses" (E 593, K 90); soon after, he etched into the plates of *The Marriage of Heaven and Hell* a paean to what he called in his exuberant phrase "enlarged & numerous senses," including the famous proclamation: "If the doors of perception were cleansed every thing would appear to man as it is, infinite" (11, 14; E 37, 39; K 153, 154).

Such apparently conflicting statements have produced a wealth of conflicting interpretations, but Robert F. Gleckner's interpretation may be the one most capable of accounting for the variety of aspects in which Blake, throughout his career, regarded the senses. According to Gleckner, the psychological unity and immediate apprehension of truth that Blake desires can be achieved "not by a destruction of the senses or reason and a substitution of imagination for them but rather by means of those senses themselves, by what Blake calls in *The Marriage* 'an improvement of sensual enjoyment,' in the prophecies the reintegration of the four Zoas."[2] When Blake speaks against "sense," then, he is really speaking against the narrow use of the senses as passive receptors rather than as organs of imaginative perception.

Blake constructed a mysticism of a new form, a mysticism with strong affinities to empirical psychology.[3] In a recent article, Joanne Witke has presented an interesting argument on the recurring topic of Blake's "empiricism."[4] She seeks to refute the analogy that is often supposed to exist between Blake's fundamental theory of knowledge and that of Neoplatonism; she emphasizes, instead, the resemblances between his epistemology and that of Berkeley and Hume. Blake obviously learned much from traditional philosophies; but, as Witke points out, he did not believe in the existence of any higher reality of supersensible forms. To Blake, all "forms" are the objects of perception. Now, there is, as Witke asserts, some similarity between Blake's ideas and Hume's: both prefer the claims of experience to those of rationalistic reflection, and both are consequently sceptical about the value of a religion of "reason" and "nature." However, the parallel that she seeks to draw between Blake's emphasis on the imagination and Hume's is not convincing; as Morton D. Paley has shown, they would not have agreed on what "imagination" is.[5]

Witke is on firmer ground in discussing the similarity between Blake's theories and Berkeley's contention that, as she puts it, "things *are* ideas and have their existence only in the mind." Similarly, Blake asserts that "Mental Things are alone Real" and that there is no "Existence Out of Mind or Thought" (*A Vision of the Last Judgment;* E 555, K 617).

One difficulty with Witke's analysis, however, is that it would be impossible to prove that Blake was consciously indebted to the radical empiricists who preceded him. His few references to Hume are negative; he labels him, idiosyncratically enough, a "Deist" and a proponent of "Newtonian Natural Religion" (*Jerusalem* 52, *Milton* 40. 13; E 199, 140; K 682, 532). Blake annotated Berkeley's *Siris*, but his notes are not very revealing of influence. He agrees with the idea that Berkeley quotes from Themistius — "all beings are in the soul" (E 654, K 775) — but he is more intent on expressing his own ideas than in focusing on Berkeley's argument.[6] *Siris* is, after all, a late and, by Berkeleian standards, rather conservative work. Geoffrey Keynes suggests that Blake annotated *Siris* sometime around 1818; Bernard Blackstone thinks that he may have read it much closer to 1800[7] — but in any event, this particular book could have had only a slight effect on the psychology that Blake had already substantially developed.

Of course, we need not expect a poet who has his symbol of imagination proclaim that he "must Create a System, or be enslav'd by another Mans" to spend much time acknowledging intellectual debts to others (*Jerusalem* 10.20; E 151, K 629). Blake's failure to acknowledge his sources greatly limits our ability to find them in any specific author, but there is no reason to insist on his total independence of his eighteenth-century predecessors or to blind ourselves to any reasonably close similarities we may find between his ideas and those that were current in his time. One may assume that Berkeley's philosophy would have come to his attention relatively early, and that he would not have found it unattractive. In any case, it is clear that Blake made use of ideas which were in his time more widely held and for which it is consequently more difficult to discover one specific source.

Blake's first attempt to formulate his own system of thought — the two tractates *There Is No Natural Religion* and *All Religions Are One* (c. 1788; E 1–3, K 97–98) — shows something of his ability to assimilate, as well as rebel against, the ideas he received from his immediate predecessors. Here Blake is seeking a sufficient psychological basis for that hoary demigod of the eighteenth century, original genius. Late-eighteenth-century aestheticians generally emphasized the importance of sensibility as a basic element of genius, and they sometimes treated sensibility as if it were an unusually refined sensitivity to normal perceptions and feelings. Viewed from Blake's perspective, this must be considered a wrong approach to the question of creativity:

> The desires & perceptions of man untaught by any thing but organs of sense, must be limited to objects of sense.
>   . . . .
> . . . If it were not for the Poetic or Prophetic character the Philosophic & Experimental would soon be at the ratio of all things, & stand still unable to do other than repeat the same dull round over again. (*No Natural Religion* a9, b11)

Although Blake is writing a critique of Lockean philosophy, it is not his purpose to deny the empiricist equation between experience and knowledge. He is always the enemy of a reductive use of "experiment," but he clearly wishes to "save" "Experimental" knowledge by finding a faculty of perception that can supply new sources of experience. Against a false theory of psychology, experience itself proves that innovation actually occurs, that thought does not, in fact, "repeat the same dull round over again." Experience is less limited than the philosophers of experience suppose: "Mans perceptions are not bounded by organs of perception. he percieves [*sic*] more than sense (tho' ever so acute) can discover" (*No Natural Religion* b3). Again, Blake is not writing against perception and experience as such, only against a narrowly limited use of them. He remains convinced that because "the true method of knowledge is experiment the true faculty of knowing must be the faculty which experiences." That faculty he identifies as the "Poetic Genius," the source of all religious and philosophical innovation, and the means by which "God becomes as we are, that we may be as he is" (*All Religions Are One* 3, 4, 6, 8; *No Natural Religion* b12).

Blake takes an ironic pleasure in attacking empiricism on its own ground, or — more accurately — in revising a form of empiricism into a form of mysticism. But in order to do so, he has to meet the challenge that empirical psychology posed to the self's integrity. If all our ideas merely reproduce, in one form or another, impressions derived from the external world, then, seemingly, we have no source of mystical knowledge — or philosophical certainty, or the radical creativity of original genius. A general solution to this problem is likely to involve either a belief in God's active influence in the self, or a belief in sources of knowledge inherent in the self but superior to common sensory perception. Despite Blake's reliance, throughout his works, on biblical symbolism and on such biblical concepts as man's fall and redemption, few of his readers would be willing to argue that a personal God, considered in isolation from human psychology, has any function in his system. Blake adopts, therefore, the second solution to the problem of the self. In doing so, he shows some affinity to less radical thinkers who preceded him. Blake's contemporaries would not have seen anything very surprising in some of the positions he takes in the tractates, particularly his attempt to rectify empirical psychology by disposing of the idea that "Man has no notion of moral fitness but from Education" (*No Natural Religion* a3). Shaftesbury, Hutcheson, and their followers had dealt with this threat to the self by positing the existence of innate internal senses or principles of feeling with powers almost as remarkable as those of Blake's new version of original genius. His reference to the Poetic Genius as "the true Man" recalls his predecessors' eagerness to identify the most useful of the mind's internal principles with the true self (*All Religions Are One* 4). Like them, Blake believes that the existence of such an autonomous self can be inferred from experiential evidence.

In addition, whether Blake at this period was consciously influenced by Berkeley or not, his attempt to assert the autonomy of the self brought him to the Berkeleian idea that perception is not dependent on external objects. Even as early as 1789, he remarked that "the Natural Earth & Atmosphere is a Phantasy" (Annotations to *Divine Love;* E 596, K 94). Just as he pushed the concepts of original genius and innate mental powers to their furthest extreme, so he converted his form of subjectivism into something even more radical than Berkeley's by omitting the God who for Berkeley was the stable source of perception. It is a short step from Blake's assertion in *There Is No Natural Religion* that "God becomes as we are, that we may be as he is" to his statement shortly later in *The Marriage of Heaven and Hell* that "All deities reside in the human breast" and that "there is no other God" but "great men" (*Marriage* 11, 23; E 37, 42; K 153, 158).

In years to come, Blake's metaphysics would assimilate scores of influences, and his symbolism would achieve a vast and redundant growth. But beneath it all, there is a stubborn adherence to basic principles. In his latest works, he still insists on the ideas and even the phrases of *The Marriage of Heaven and Hell:*

> the Worship of God, is honouring his gifts
> In other men: & loving the greatest men best, each according
> To his Genius: which is the Holy Ghost in Man; there is no other
> God, than that God who is the intellectual fountain of Humanity.
> (*Jerusalem* 91.7–10; E 248, K 738)

David Wagenknecht observes in his commentary on this passage that "it is useful to be reminded, in the face of so much talk about Blake's 'renovated Christianity,' of [the] heterodoxy" of his opinions.[8] Just as Blake used Christian concepts, and turned them to his own purposes, so also he used a variety of esoteric symbols and ideas; the extent and nature of such borrowings may never be precisely determined. Yet if Blake's thought — and, in particular, his basic theory of psychology — were merely the rusted remains of various esoteric systems, it would in fact be little more than the quaint aberration it is often unjustly considered to be. Despite his aversion to post-Lockean thought, he made a serious attempt to solve the problems of the self that had been raised by empirical philosophy; and despite his failure to acknowledge his relationship to some of his eighteenth-century predecessors, he sharpened a number of their intellectual weapons in order to wage his own "Mental Fight."

I will have occasion to comment further on similarities between Blake and his predecessors. But there is a more intriguing question: Is Blake's radically "individualist" psychology a real solution to the problems he addressed?[9] The answer, I think, is that it is not. No adequate theory of the self can be built on the principle of Poetic Genius, which, as I take it, lies at the heart of Blake's philosophy. His theory of psychology was, perhaps, influenced only slightly more by his belief in an essential "true Man" than by the necessity of avoiding the difficulties implicit in that belief.

Blake's philosophy is incapable of providing a consistent concept of personal identity, and this is true despite his constant emphasis on free expression of individuality. Creative genius, according to his annotations to Joshua Reynolds' *Discourses*, is wholly individual: "I do not believe that Rafael taught Mich. Angelo or that Mich. Ang: taught Rafael., any more than I believe that the Rose teaches the Lilly how to grow or the Apple tree teaches the Pear tree how to bear Fruit. I do not believe the tales of Anecdote writers when they militate against Individual Character" (E 632, K 453). But is genius really an individuating principle? In *All Religions Are One*, Blake initially suggests that it is when he calls it the "true Man."[10] But by the end of the tractate, the "true Man" is no longer simply an inhabitant of the individual mind but a "universal Poetic Genius" which is responsible for the similarities in "Religeons [*sic*] of all Nations" (7–10). Blake makes his transition from the individual to the universal by observing that "as all men are alike in outward form, So (and with the same infinite variety) all are alike in the Poetic Genius" (5) — an observation that raises more questions than it answers.

Blake's problem here is one more version of the eighteenth-century dilemma of identity versus significance: the more individual any psychological principle appears to be, the less significance it may appear to have. Of what significance is individual creativity if it is not intimately related to a larger order? In *All Religions Are One*, Blake tries to escape from this difficulty by implying that in essence the Poetic Genius is always the same, although in practice it may manifest itself in different ways. Such ideas also appear in the annotations that he wrote about the same time to Lavater's *Aphorisms on Man*. In the annotations it is evident that, despite Blake's abhorrence of "abstract reason," he was not above an occasional reliance on the rationalistic habit of abstracting "essences." Lavater's first and second aphorisms, which Blake approves as "true Christian philosophy far above all abstraction," are similar to Blake's argument in the tractate:

1. Know, in the first place, that mankind agree in essence, as they do in their limbs and senses.
2. Mankind differ as much in essence as they do in form, limbs, and senses—and only so, and not more.[11]

These aphorisms tell us very little about what a man's essence may be, or about how much mankind "agree" or "differ." But when Lavater, in his third aphorism, refers to the self's habit of imagining that it is "the centre of being," Blake remarks: "It is the God in *all* that is our companion & friend. . . . our Lord is the word of God & every thing on earth is the word of God & in its essence is God" (E 572–73, 588–89; K 65, 87).[12]

This is the characteristic movement of Blake's thought, from microcosm to macrocosm, from self to Man to God. Clearly, this movement proceeds from a desire to confer the utmost spiritual significance upon the essential self. But the idea that the self, like everything else, is in "essence" God provides no basis for exploring the question of identity that otherwise seems so important to Blake. It does no good for him to tell us, in his comments on Swedenborg's notion of God's identity, that "Essence is not Identity but from Essence proceeds Identity & from one Essence may proceed many Identities. . . . If the Essence was the same *as the* Identity there could be but one Identity. which is false" (Annotations to *Divine Love*; E 593, K 91). We still do not know in what identity consists.

But one fact is certain: in theory, at least, Blake would never have agreed with Hume that "mankind . . . are nothing but a bundle or collection of different perceptions." In practice, especially in analyzing fallen man, Blake was capable of contradicting his theory; and later I will cite some instances of Blake as a "Humean" psychologist. In *A Vision of the Last Judgment*, however, he emphasizes the intransigence of identity: "In Eternity one Thing never Changes into another Thing Each Identity is Eternal." But what is true of Eternity is not necessarily true of the fallen world: "Eternal Identity is one thing & Corporeal Vegetation is another thing." In the fallen world, at least, eternal identity is involved in the vicissitudes of the eternal "states" of innocence, experience, and so forth: "Man Passes on but States remain for Ever he passes thro them like a traveller. . . . Every Thing is Eternal" (E 546, K 606, 607). In *Jerusalem,* Blake insists on the importance of a continual exchange of a lower for a higher identity, or at least perception of identity: "Man is born a Spectre or Satan & is altogether an Evil, & requires a New Selfhood continually & must continually be changed into his direct Contrary" (52; E 198, K 682).

Above this passage in *Jerusalem* appear these words: "The Spiritual States of the Soul are all Eternal[.] Distinguish between the Man, & his present State." But although Blake wishes us to do so, it is very difficult to distinguish the "eternal identities" in his works from the "eternal states" through which they pass. Since it is imagination, the Poetic Genius or "true Man," that allows the self to escape into Eternity, one would expect individual imagination, the godlike essence, to form the basis of identity. But in order to give imagination the highest possible significance, Blake describes it as superpersonal, eternally renewing itself in roughly the same way in successive men. In *A Vision of the Last Judgment,* he allows for the fact that "to different People" an imaginative vision "appears differently as every thing else does for tho on Earth things seem Permanent they are less permanent than a Shadow." Yet he continues in this way:

The Nature of Visionary Fancy or Imagination is very little Known & the Eternal nature & permanence of its ever Existent Images is considerd as less permanent than the things of Vegetative & Generative Nature yet the Oak dies as well as the Lettuce but Its Eternal Image & Individuality never dies.but renews by its seed. just so the Imaginative Image returns by the seed of Contemplative Thought. (E 544–45, K 605)

This says something about the persistence of the "Imaginative Image," but it hardly explains how either one genius or one self can be considered eternally distinct from another. One suspects that it is really the earthly state through which the self is currently passing that gives it and its visions individual character.[13] Whether Blake pictures his characters as locked in static roles or subject to erratic change, their identities generally appear as little more than qualities acquired in combat with a fallen existence.

It is routine among Blake's critics to remark what Margaret Lowery once called the "strange absence of personalities" in his poems. Mark Schorer properly discounted the explanation that Blake was simply "deficient in the descriptive imagination" — an explanation that could be disproved by any of a hundred passages in Blake's works. The problem, Schorer suggests, is that Blake

seems really to have submitted to that very tendency to generalize and idealize for which he never ceased to upbraid his contemporaries. He may have thought that he was expressing "essences," yet the fact is that his "essences" are at least as devoid of particularity as those fixed and final norms which the eighteenth century hoped to discover under the flux and shadows of temporal and local accident.[14]

Schorer is referring to Blake's personification of essential psychological principles, but Blake also frequently describes his characters as if they were nothing but essential states of experience.

Strictly speaking, Blake's mythological creatures — Los, Urizen, and their associates — are not autonomous identities but broken fragments of an eternal, universal identity which he calls in *Jerusalem* the "Eternal Individuality" of the Giant Albion (48.3; E 194, K 677). As H. M. Margoliouth has observed, the Zoas and their emanations "are not persons but recurrent elements of the soul which change their character and activity according to the action of other elements and the degree of their 'fall.' "[15] In fact, the Zoas give a new drama and dignity to the internal forces of the self; they represent the furthest development of the eighteenth-century "sublime." The ennobling effect of sublimity had often been ascribed to the mind's ability to internalize its setting, but in Blake's mythology the cosmos is internalized completely, or, rather, exists from the beginning as a property of mind — macrocosm read in its entirety into microcosm.

Physical space becomes illusion, while the expansive mental space imagined by earlier poets of the sublime becomes the only reality. Blake's mythological characters are of course capable of acquiring meanings on many levels, and we often have reason to be concerned with them as individuals who enact roles similar to those we find in the states of real life. It is largely because they are capable of being viewed in this manner that the Zoas attain their dramatic interest, and it is because of this that they are able to symbolize a social psychology as well as a psychology of the private self. Yet this brings up a problem: the Zoas really appear as fully distinct "selves" only to the extent that they are detached and limited portions of Eternity, but one is expected to measure their spiritual significance by the degree to which they attain a more or less advanced state of reintegration into the eternal Whole. In analyzing Blake's works, one is confronted with an issue that arises frequently in the interpretation of Romantic literature. The so-called Romantic impulse toward union with nature or some other universal process has often been explained as a flight from the limitations of self and self-consciousness, yet it may also be interpreted as the natural result of a desire to affirm the self's significance by making the self an organic part of something vastly greater. The danger in this is that one may begin to lose interest in the individual self except as it aspires to union with the Whole.

In constructing his account of man's reintegration as a social organism, Blake showed his awareness of this problem by trying to depict mankind restored to "humanity" as an intimate union of independent beings, each of them a "Minute Particular" contributing significance and "vitality" to the whole with which it is united (*Jerusalem* 91.28–30; E 249, K 738). But throughout his career, Blake had difficulty handling the concept of personal identity, and this was mainly because he had difficulty defining the self's relation to the external world. Difficulties of this kind had plagued British philosophy and literature throughout the eighteenth century, and it is not surprising that Blake's attempted solutions to the general problem sometimes look much like previous solutions. In his annotations to Reynolds, he falls back on the belief that something is born within the self that makes it independent of the outside world: "Knowledge

of Ideal Beauty. is Not to be Acquired It is Born with us Innate
Ideas. are in Every Man Born with him. they are truly Himself. The
Man who says that we have No Innate Ideas must be a Fool &
Knave. Having No Con-Science or Innate Science" (E 637, K 459).
By using the old term "innate ideas," Blake seemingly associates
himself with pre-Lockean psychology. But as usual, one must exercise more than normal caution with Blake's terminology. As Northrop Frye points out, Locke denied "what from Blake's point of
view would be innate generalizations, and Blake does not believe in
them any more than Locke does."[16] Taken in the context of the rest
of Blake's thought, his notion of "innate ideas" has less to do with
positive concepts than with two mental qualities to which he has
just alluded in his attack on Reynolds: innate "Inspiration" and the
"Enthusiastic Admiration" that he calls "the first Principle of Knowledge & its last" (E 636, K 458). Blake's innate ideas are really the innate disposition to be inspired with vision and to form correct intuitive judgments. Again, in this respect his psychological theory
seems closer to the theories of Shaftesbury — and Hutcheson, and
Kames — than to those of the pre-Lockeans.[17] The important difference is that Blake assigns the controlling power of intuition to the
creative imagination rather than to a moral or aesthetic sense: "All
Forms are Perfect in the Poets Mind. but these are not Abstracted
nor Compounded from Nature but are from Imagination" (E 637, K
459). The principles of genius and imagination are, in Blake's metaphor, "seeds" planted in the mind at birth (E 645–46, K 471).

The seed, however, is not the flower; and a person's internal principle of imagination cannot be regarded as "truly," and exclusively,
"Himself" unless one denies that the external world nourishes the
self. Blake added to his theory of imaginative genius the Berkeleian
concept that the external world is really contained within the mind,
but he appears to have been somewhat hesitant, especially during
the early part of his career, about whether this concept of psychic
autonomy is really an adequate solution to the problem of the self.
In his annotations to Lavater he is attracted to a different position:

Man is bad or good. as he unites himself with bad or good spirits. tell me
with whom you go & Ill tell you what you do

. . . we cannot experience pleasure but by means of others who experience either pleasure or pain thro us. . . . all of us on earth are united in thought, for it is impossible to think without images of somewhat on earth. (E 589–90, K 88)

Here Blake seems almost prepared to adopt the assumption, often to be found in the eighteenth century, that significant experience is social and sympathetic, that thought subsists on impressions of the external world that necessarily mold each individual into an intellectual similarity with others. Any rigorous application of this principle would destroy the rest of Blake's beliefs, but a semblance of it lingers in his descriptions of the "self-closd," spectrous Urizen who, because he is "self-contemplating," naturally contemplates only a "void" (*Book of Urizen* 3–4; E 69–71, K 222–24).

It would be difficult — perhaps impossible — to reconcile all the contradictions that appeared in Blake's psychological theory as it evolved. It seems evident, however, that he opposes solipsism when it is the product of rationalistic "reflection" but not when it is the product of imaginative "vision." He is not concerned so much with the ultimate question of whether the external world exists as with the immediate question of how well we perceive whatever world there is. In this connection, a letter that Blake wrote to Dr. John Trusler on August 23, 1799, is worth examining closely:

I see Every thing I paint In This World, but Every body does not see alike. To the Eyes of a Miser a Guinea is more beautiful than the Sun & a bag worn with the use of Money has more beautiful proportions than a Vine filled with Grapes. The tree which moves some to tears of joy is in the Eyes of others only a Green thing that stands in the way. Some See Nature all Ridicule & Deformity & by these I shall not regulate my proportions, & Some Scarce see Nature at all But to the Eyes of the Man of Imagination Nature is Imagination itself. As a man is So he Sees. . . . To Me This World is all One continued Vision of Fancy or Imagination. (E 677, K 793)

Blake had an active contempt for Trusler's intellect, and in writing to him he made a conscientious effort to reduce his own ideas to their simplest form. Stated in this way, they seem less like the Perennial Philosophy than a rather advanced version of the principle of selective perception, the idea that, for better or worse, the self necessarily chooses and modifies its perceptions to make them conform with its own character. The mind's ability to interpret its perceptions in its own way had caused doubts among empirical philosophers about the possibility of objective knowledge, but Blake makes the principle of selective perception, which could so easily lead to scepticism, a basis of his mystical philosophy. Yet he saw that a faith, not merely in the existence, but also in the independent value of purely individual habits of perception is necessary to any systematic theory of original genius. Earlier theorists, restrained by a need to place genius in a context of significance founded on its participation in the common feelings of humanity, often failed to make this connection, but Blake did not.

Blake's confidence in his own unique habits of perception affected his poetry in very obvious ways. The unique vision that saw the forms of a new mythology in the fallen powers of the individual mind was also the solipsistic rapture that saw the makings of apocalypse in the obscure quarrels of William Hayley, poetaster, and William Blake, engraver. By basing his poetic almost entirely on subjective vision, Blake denied himself any external standard by which to evaluate the relative merits of his acts of self-expression. Vision must be tested by vision alone.[18]

The objection may be made that in the Trusler letter Blake himself distinguishes the vision of "joy" from the vision — or mere sight — of "Deformity," thereby establishing an effective criterion for valuing one mode of perception above another. It should be noticed, however, that Blake's distinction between the two modes is in essence a moral or even a pragmatic one: the imaginative man is simply better, happier, or more "integrated" than the unimaginative man. This is still, of course, a reason for valuing one condition above another; we would all choose to be citizens of Eternity rather than denizens of Ulro. The real problem is that the self is conversant only with perceptions that mirror itself and can therefore have no truly objective knowledge of its own condition. The person who sees a tree as only a "Green thing" has no way of knowing that he should see it as anything different. Immediate perception, not objective evaluation, convinces the visionary that his "fancies" are true, at least for him. In morals, likewise, Blake trusts the spontaneous impulses of the individual "conscience" as the source of truth (Annotations to Richard Watson's *Apology*; E 603, K 385–86).

In his epics, Blake sets himself the task of describing man's ascent from fallen, "natural" perception to full imaginative vision. The effort required all of Blake's resources of creative vision and rhetorical ingenuity. It is difficult to imagine, clearly and systematically, how that redemptive process could take place on the individual, psychological level, if only because the fallen self can have no knowledge of any state to which it should aspire. Inspiration can hardly come from the outside; generally speaking, the actors in Blake's epics are aspects, projections, faculties, or principles of the self. The self must therefore act spontaneously, automatically — as automatically as Blake himself acted when, as he claimed, he wrote "an immense number of verses" from "immediate Dictation," under a mysterious duress.[19] This is perhaps one reason why Blake's narration is often not an orderly movement from sufficient cause to probable effect but a series of somewhat desperate leaps from one sudden decision of his giant forms to another.[20]

In this connection it is interesting to observe the way in which Blake handles the problem of psychological motivation in two of his early works, *The Book of Thel* and *Visions of the Daughters of Albion*, in each of which the self is offered the chance to progress to a new state of existence. Although Thel listens patiently enough to a number of arguments for advancing into the world of experience, she is unable to take the appropriate action. But in *Visions of the Daughters of Albion*, Oothoon listens for a moment to the flower of Leutha's vale and spontaneously obeys her own desire, suggested by the flower, to become a new self capable of mature sexuality. Later, however, when she attempts to convince Theotormon that he also can achieve a higher form of life, he remains unmoved by her arguments because he is incapable of destroying his self-limiting habits of perception. In Blake's world, progress normally happens spontaneously or not at all. To the extent that they can be considered "selves," his characters are often effectively isolated from the external world and can advance only when impelled by internal forces as mysterious as they are sudden. Blake's characters frequently do not so much affect one another as indulge in mutual displays of self-absorption.

But like most of the issues that arise in Blake's poetry, this question of personality and motivation is far from simple. As Helen T. McNeil has observed in connection with *The Four Zoas*, Blake's characters can often be said to act spontaneously "according to the requirements of the present situation, not according to a concept of stable personality"; *The Four Zoas* is in fact "an epic of situations."[21] This is not quite what one might expect from Blake's individualist principles; it is somewhat ironic, especially in view of what I have said about the prevalence of situations rather than fully analyzed characters in much of the earlier literature of feeling. The Zoas may in effect *become* the situations to which they react, yet they are not, finally, reacting to anything "external," anything outside the mind. This is the poetry of pure psychology, pure "feeling"; but it is very nearly the reduction and disposal of any psychology that connects the self with actual events.

This is not to deny the instances in which Blake frees his characters from their native solipsism and allows them to affect each other profoundly. But in such cases their interaction often turns out to be a sorry and degraded thing. Despite his belief in "eternal identities," his psychology is based on a theory of perception — imaginative or otherwise — and he often virtually equates the self with its perceptions: "Strucken with Albions disease they become what they behold; / They assimilate with Albion in pity & compassion" (*Jerusalem* 39.32–33; E 185, K 674). This is one respect in which Blake, at least in practice, resembles his predecessors Hume and Smith. When he admits the possibility of full human interaction, he tends, as they did, to regard it as a process in which one self is likely to be transformed by its perceptions of another self. As one might expect, in describing the fallen world Blake generally views this process as something that deprives the self of its capacity for spontaneous aspiration to a higher mental state. In "The Mental Traveller," the fingers of the Woman Old "number every Nerve" of the male Babe; by controlling his perceptions, she can control his identity, or rather try to exchange her identity for his: "She grows young as he grows old" (ll. 17, 20; E 475, K 425). The poem suggests that identities can be traded and subverted thus in an endless cycle without either self experiencing final imaginative rebirth. Blake's idea that the character of the self is connected with the character of its perceptions allows just as much for a self-subverting "outer" vision as for a creative "inner" vision. The difference is that in Blake's poetry the process by which the self is subverted by its perceptions sometimes appears to have a logic and inevitability that is lacking in the spontaneous, virtually causeless process by which the self attains a higher state of imaginative vision.

But this is probably more than enough Urizenic dissection of Blake's ideas. His philosophy of the self fails to resolve a number of the problems to which it is addressed, but it offers penetrating analyses of some of the failures of other philosophies. This is particularly true of Blake's criticism of the concepts of sympathy and sensibility that were basic to most of the psychological, ethical, and aesthetic theories of his time. Although he could not avoid assigning great importance to the self's capacity to be transformed by its sensibility to other selves, he ordinarily regarded sympathy and sensibility — as they were commonly understood — as negative principles at enmity with creative genius and the essential self. When Wordsworth lists sensibility among the powers necessary to the production of poetry, Blake replies: "One Power alone makes a Poet. — Imagination The Divine Vision" (Annotations to Wordsworth's *Poems;* E 654, K 782).

Blake's ideas on the subject of sympathy, sensibility, pity, and other related concepts are as complex as any other element of his thought. Annotating Lavater in 1788, he records his agreement with the highly conventional idea that "all great minds sympathize" and that the ability to "transpose [one]self into another's situation" is saintly (E 588, 586; K 86, 84). A little later, however, in *The Marriage of Heaven and Hell*, he pictures sympathy as the emotion that a baboon affects while devouring another baboon (20; E 41, K 157). On a page of *The Four Zoas* he scribbles the epigram, "Till thou dost injure the distrest / Thou shalt never have peace within thy breast," next to a powerful image of sympathy and solipsism united in the fallen mind:

> Beyond the bounds of their own self their senses cannot penetrate
> As the tree knows not what is outside of its leaves & bark
> And yet it drinks the summer joy & fears the winter sorrow
> So in the regions of the grave none knows his dark compeer
> Tho he partakes of his dire woes & mutual returns the pang
> The throb the dolor the convulsion in soul sickening woes[.]
>
> (p. 70, ll. 12–17; E 340, 754, K 314, 380)

In *Jerusalem*, Blake is a strangely militant advocate of "pity" and "forgiveness of sin." Yet it must be admitted that even here he is far from approving any very conventional idea of sympathy and pity as moral virtues. Earlier, in *Europe*, Blake had shown that he could be a moral iconoclast without being a moral nihilist; there he regrets that the dreaming ages of false religion have "chang'd . . . that which pitieth: / To a devouring flame" even while he is satirizing Urizen for "feeding his soul with pity" (10.16–17, 12.4; E 62, 63; K 241, 242). He had made it obvious, in the *Songs of Innocence and Experience*, that he viewed a pure form of sympathy as a primary characteristic of the state of innocence, just as he considered a perverted form of sympathy or pity a characteristic of the state of experience.[22]

   Much of the power of Blake's poetry comes from his ability to find the full horror or beauty implicit in psychological theories that other authors might regard merely as "explanations" to be accepted or rejected. Out of the concept of sympathy, Blake develops images of a delightful, if ultimately limited, tenderness; but he also develops visions of terror and alienation. One of the most dramatic examples of the latter is the scene in *The Book of Urizen* in which Los is "divided / Before the death-image of Urizen." Viewing Urizen's horrible condition in his fall from Eternity,

> Los wept obscur'd with mourning:
> His bosom earthquak'd with sighs;
> He saw Urizen deadly black,
> In his chains bound, & Pity began,

> In anguish dividing & dividing
> For pity divides the soul
> In pangs eternity on eternity
> Life in cataracts pourd down his cliffs
> The void shrunk the lymph into Nerves
> Wand'ring wide on the bosom of night
> And left a round globe of blood
> Trembling upon the Void[.]
>
> (15.1–2, 13.48–59; E 77, 76; K 230)

In this scene, it is clear that Blake's resistance to conventional concepts of pity and sympathy is of central importance in defining the psychological dimension of his metaphysic of the fallen world. Here we are not dealing merely with the hypocritical sympathy that Blake continually denounces; Los's reaction to what he sees is honest and, in fact, perfectly understandable. But the sympathy he feels is of a kind that Blake also consistently opposes — the "pity" that "divides the soul."

In Harold Bloom's words, Los becomes "the image of the death he pities, and so divides his being in two."[23] Here, as in so many other eighteenth-century and Romantic descriptions of the sympathetic self, there is the suggestion of a mirror image, of the self reflecting what it sees in the outside world as it sympathetically conforms to its perceptions.[24] Earlier in this study, I noted some of the difficulties that seem to be inherent in the concept of sympathetic identification and in the imagery of mirrors it implies. In *Urizen*, Blake satirizes the idea that sympathetic identification ennobles the self, expands it, or shows it, by reflection, its real nature. Los's sympathetic reaction conforms to the conventions established in eighteenth-century philosophy and literature: he responds automatically to Urizen's plight, he adopts the proper emotional attitude of pity, and he apparently seeks the object of his pity with vibrating nerves that literally, not just metaphorically, extend his feeling beyond the boundaries of his self. His pity finally assumes the form of a separate person — a woman, appropriately enough, since writers of sensibility commonly considered women peculiarly susceptible to such tender and delicate emotions. The Eternals, however, "call'd her Pity, and fled"; they flee in terror of the emotionally divided self as well as of the division of genders that proceeds from it (19.1; E 77, K 231).

Los has become a mirror of Urizen's fallen condition, but he has not simply *become* Urizen; no theory of sympathy implied that he could. He has, however, internalized enough of what he sees to destroy the singleness of his identity and deprive himself of the power to act creatively. Los bears some resemblance to the hero of sensibility, the kind of hero Mackenzie saw in Hamlet — a character whose feelings make him "a sort of double person." Mackenzie finds an "indescribable charm" in the impotence and perplexity of the double-selfed hero of personality;[25] Blake, the apostle of creative action, emphatically does not. The basic notion of the self as ideally yielding and "ductile" is repellent to him. This position, almost as much as his opposition to what he considers a reductive use of reason, distinguishes Blake's psychology from that of his eighteenth-century predecessors. In his view, sympathy may be freely given to deserving objects — as it is in the *Songs of Innocence* — but it should not become a direct determinant of personal identity.

As I have suggested previously, an unexamined faith in sympathy and sensibility may, in fact, lead to a kind of reductionism. In late-eighteenth-century literature, a few references to a character's capacity for sympathy, pity, and the other sentimental virtues are sometimes regarded as an adequate delineation of his identity. In treatises on the arts, a few general remarks on sensibility are sometimes considered a sufficient account of some of the most important powers of genius. All of this was only natural in an age in which an innate capacity for the social and sentimental virtues was often almost equated, in popular philosophy, with the "true self." Blake rejected this confusion of psychology with morality, this lack of interest in psychological diversity and complexity. He argues that "Goodness or Badness has nothing to do with Character. an Apple tree a Pear tree a Horse a Lion, are Characters but a Good Apple tree or a Bad, is an Apple tree still: a Horse is not more a Lion for being a Bad Horse. that is its Character: its Goodness or Badness is another consideration" (*On Homer's Poetry*; E 267, K 778). In *The*

Marriage of Heaven and Hell, Blake describes a capacity for what is traditionally known as virtue as merely one of the dynamic contraries existing within the self:

> Without Contraries is no progression. Attraction and Repulsion, Reason and Energy, Love and Hate, are necessary to Human existence.
> From these contraries spring what the religious call Good & Evil. (3; E 34, K 149)

Eighteenth-century thinkers often begin their works as psychologists investigating the individual self, but having discovered there some capacity for "benevolence" or "sympathy," they readily become moralists prescribing general systems of ethics based upon that capacity. What such systems lose in rigor of psychological analysis they make up for in moral purpose — and, as Blake saw it, in demands for moral and psychological conformism. These are Urizen's demands, which begin with "laws of peace, of love, of unity: / Of pity, compassion, forgiveness" but end with

> One command, one joy, one desire,
> One curse, one weight, one measure
> One King, one God, one Law.
> *(Book of Urizen* 4.34–40; E 71, K 224)

Blake is, of course, thinking primarily about the Old Testament Jehovah, whom he regarded as a ruthless but well-intentioned tyrant; but his attack is also directed against Christian and post-Christian attempts to found a conformist ethic on the sentimental virtues.[26]

Urizen's ideal of social harmony ironically proceeds from meditations in "the depths of dark solitude" (4.6; E 70, K 224). As a student of history, Blake is commenting on the megalomania that has often inspired the promulgation of coercive law; as a student of psychology, he is emphasizing the fact that a desire to establish sympathetic "unity" with other people sometimes proceeds from a narrow and unhealthy absorption in self — in the type of "selfhood" he always opposes. "The Mental Traveller" contains Blake's most telling statement of this seeming paradox. The exposed sensibilities of his characters allow them to achieve a kind of unity, a kind of "sympathy" with each other, but the process resembles combat as much as love. Identities are constantly being transformed, conformed to each other, yet the motive on each side is self-aggrandizement, the desire to "plant" oneself in another's "Nerves," to make another person one's "dwelling place" (ll. 25–28; E 476, K 425). At one point, Blake's male figure is transformed into a parody of the Man of Sensibility. He is rich in the treasures of sentiment:

> the gems of the Human Soul
> The rubies & pearls of a lovesick eye
> The countless gold of the akeing heart
> The martyrs groan & the lovers sigh
>
> They are his meat they are his drink
> He feeds the Beggar & the Poor
> And the wayfaring Traveller
> For ever open is his door[.]   (ll. 33–40; E 476, K 425)

For the Host, social sympathy creates a respectable social identity, but the feast of Urizenic sentiment is merely a cannibal banquet of one self upon another.[27] The guests feed upon the Host — "His grief is their eternal joy" (l. 41) — while he feeds himself with pathetic sentiments. He adopts the conventional wisdom represented in such works as Gray's *Ode to Adversity:* the self is ennobled by sympathy, adversity, the pathos of frustrated desire; these are truly "the gems of the Human Soul."[28] But as Blake describes him, the sympathetic Host is a parallel to the Woman Old, who earlier "live[d] upon his shrieks & cries" (l. 19). She was a sadist; he has become a masochist — and, perhaps, a sadist as well. Both are emotional predators. At the moment, the Host can be neither a "lover" nor a "martyr," but he uses sympathy for his own and others' misfortunes as a means of exalting himself.

In *Visions of the Daughters of Albion,* Oothoon cries for "Love! free as the mountain wind!" — for sexual love, and not for Urizenic sentiment (7.16; E 49, K 194). The eighteenth century was not ignorant of the fact that sensibility may bear a strong relation to sensuality; the relation is made fairly explicit in Goethe's *Werther,* in Laclos' *Liaisons Dangereuses,* and even in Richardson's portrayal of

Lovelace in *Clarissa*. But for most people who believed in the ethical value of sensibility, sensuality remained the dark side of the self. Of course, the major reason why sensibility was assumed to have ethical value in the first place is that it seemed to represent a potential for broad social sympathy and sensitivity to established social values. But for Blake, it is the sense of touch that is the most important aspect of man's general "sensibility." Through the eyes one can "see small portions of the eternal world," but through the sexual sense of touch one can "pass out" into that world. But people prefer not to enhance themselves by enjoying their sexual sensibility honestly: "For stolen joys are sweet, & bread eaten in secret pleasant" (*Europe* iii. 3–6; E 58–59, K 237). To Blake, repression of hedonic sensibility in favor of social sensibility or delicacy seemed to lie at the root of the Urizenic code of virtue.

In Blake's vision of regeneration, male principles unite with their separated female emanations, and each of the four Zoas unites with the others, all impelled to union by a sublime sympathy. Yet Blake's emphasis on the ideally free and assertive self, whose identity is finally irreducible, makes this concept of "sympathy" something different from the concepts of his eighteenth-century predecessors. The sympathy that reunites male and female principles is primarily an attraction between different parts of the self; and when we consider Blake's idea of regained unity in its social as well as its personal aspect, we will not find Blake relying on any notion of sympathy as the basis of conventional social rules. Los, in fact, denounces the "Heavens" based on "Law" as antithetical to what he calls "sympathy" and "benevolence." He describes those Heavens as

> Swelld & bloated General Forms, repugnant to the Divine-
> Humanity, who is the Only General and Universal Form
> To which all Lineaments tend & seek with love & sympathy[.]
> All broad & general principles belong to benevolence
> Who protects minute particulars, every one in their own identity.
>
> (*Jerusalem* 38.18–23; E 183, K 672)

In this vision of spiritual sympathy and benevolence which involve minute particulars in the Divine Humanity, Blake is perhaps indebted to some of the concepts, as well as the vocabulary, of the philosophers of sympathy; but one may be badly misled by failing to distinguish Blake's usage from theirs. His idea of social reintegration is the opposite, not only of the Hobbesian Leviathan, but also of the eighteenth-century moral theories based on self-restraint and social sympathy.[29] The process of social redemption requires the presence of Jerusalem, who "is called Liberty among the Children of Albion"; regeneration of society requires full expression of each person's identity (*Jerusalem* 54.5; E 201, K 684). If anyone "wishes to see a Vision; a perfect Whole," Los says, he must "see it in its Minute Particulars":

> General Forms have their vitality in Particulars: & every
> Particular is a Man; a Divine Member of the Divine Jesus.
> (*Jerusalem* 91.20–21, 29–30; E 249, K 738)

When, in his later works, Blake advocates "self-annihilation," he is adopting a vocabulary similar to that of some of his eighteenth-century predecessors; and in Blake, as in Hartley, the phrase implies transcendence of a *limited* self. The paradox of losing the self in order to find it is expressed in Blake's use of a double terminology: "selfhood" for the negative and restrictive aspects of the self; "identity," "individuality," and so forth, for various aspects of the "real and immortal Self" (*Milton* 15.11; E 108, K 496). But the resemblance between Hartley and Blake cannot be traced very far. Blake's idea of self-surrender is a willingness to give up old habits of perception and submit to the imaginative visions of the true, inner man. In the words of Blake's Milton:

> To bathe in the Waters of Life; to wash off the Not Human
> I come in Self-annihilation & the grandeur of Inspiration
> To cast off Rational Demonstration by Faith in the Saviour
> To cast off the rotten rags of Memory by Inspiration
> To cast off Bacon, Locke & Newton from Albions covering
> To take off his filthy garments, & clothe him with Imagination.
> (*Milton* 41.1–6; E 141, K 533)

In Hartley, as in Blake, self-surrender may be interpreted as a peculiar form of self-assertion. In Blake, however, it is clearly an aggressive affirmation of an essential self, a strict inspection of one's "Eternal Lineaments" to determine what is "Annihilable" and what is in fact "Eternal" (*Milton* 32.30–31; E 131, K 522).[30]

Because Blake insists on both the ideal autonomy and the ideal unity of human "particulars" as a solution to the problem of personal identity, his philosophy of the self will probably always elude definitive interpretation. But it seems certain that his final emphasis is on the creative energy of each "minute particular," each "identity," and not on what anyone else would be much inclined to call "sympathy" or "benevolence." In Eternity, these two qualities exist simultaneously with "the two Sources of Life . . . Hunting and War," yet eternal sympathy is as far removed from the "natural" sympathy of this world as the sublime sports of war and hunting are from their cruel earthly counterparts (*Jerusalem* 38.31; E 183, K 672).

Writing of the affairs of the fallen world in "The Mental Traveller," Blake showed that he was sceptical not only about the ethical value of sympathy but also about the possibility of using sympathy as a means of escaping spiritual "solitude" and establishing real communion with other selves. As I have shown, Adam Smith revealed one of the weak points in the philosophy of sympathy when he admitted that we can comprehend others' feelings only by means of the imagination; we cannot enter into them directly because we can know only what we ourselves perceive. By imparting an ethical value to the imagination, this concept of sympathy contributed much to the development of literary theory; its full effects can be seen in Shelley's *Defence of Poetry*. But to the extent that imagination expresses the self, "sympathetic imagination" may be as self-regarding as Cowper's identification with the Castaway or Wordsworth's "egotistical" sympathy for some of his own characters. Despite his advocacy of self-expression, Blake believed that a tendency to convert the outside world into a mirror of the self should not be confused with real emotional communion with other selves. The Nurse in *Songs of Experience* supposes that she sympathizes with others when she is actually sympathizing with herself. The children she watches over remind her of her lost youth, and she therefore imagines that her situation is theirs and that their feelings should resemble hers:

When the voices of children, are heard on the green
And whisprings are in the dale:
The days of my youth rise fresh in my mind,
My face turns green and pale.

Then come home my children, the sun is gone down
And the dews of night arise
Your spring & your day, are wasted in play
And your winter and night in disguise.

("Nurse's Song"; E 23, K 212)

Nothing but the Nurse's own experience tells her that the children's lives will be "wasted in play" or "disguise." She is the one who is in disguise, even from herself; she unconsciously covers a selfish absorption in her own frustrations with a mask of sympathy. In verses I have previously quoted, Edward Young writes: "Like *Milton's Eve*, when gazing on the lake, / Man makes the matchless image, man admires." Blake would add that when man gazes at his own image projected upon the outside world, he may also see a reflection of himself that he despises, fears, and must reject.[31]

There is an act of imagination involved in the Nurse's projection of her own situation upon the children's. Yet this type of reversed sympathy is not really imaginative in Blake's sense, because it is not an act of creation but merely a reverie on things-as-they-are. Elsewhere he makes a similar objection to the "unselfish" sympathy that actually transforms the self into the image of what it beholds. Deep in the solitary Vales of Har, according to Blake's myth, dwell Har and Heva, a pair of aged and virtually mindless innocents. If S. Foster Damon's intuition is correct, they may represent, among other things, Blake's view of the "decadent" art of his time.[32] Certainly they are people of sensibility: "Har and Heva fled. / Because their brethren & sisters liv'd in War & Lust" (*Song of Los* 4.5–6; E 66, K 246). Their own sports are strictly humanitarian; they spend their time "playing with flowers. & running after birds," and when they catch the birds they do not kill them but only "gather them ripe cherries" (*Tiriel* 2.8, 3.13; E 274, 276; K 100, 102). They act benevolently toward the unpleasant Tiriel:

God bless thy poor bald pate. God bless. thy hollow winking eyes
God bless thy shriveld beard. God. bless. thy many wrinkled forehead
Thou hast no teeth old man & thus I kiss thy sleek bald head.

(Tiriel 2.32–34; E 275, K 101)

Like Urizen, Har and Heva seek "a joy without pain," and they attempt to make their own limitations into universal laws *(Book of Urizen* 4.10; E 70, K 224; *Tiriel* 8.7–28; E 281–82, K 109–10). Their narrow view of human life is suggested by what their nurse Mnetha exclaims when Tiriel breaks in upon their static existence: "O Lord . . . how I tremble are there then more people / More human creatures on this earth beside the sons of Har[?]" *(Tiriel* 2.48–49; E 275, K 102). But one of Blake's illustrations to *Tiriel* offers another insight into their characters (see illustration). Har and Heva bathe together in a murky forest pool. They embrace — arms floating in the same languid gesture, faces pressed together grotesquely, Har's eye staring directly into Heva's. They are totally sympathetic with each other, totally one. Each is a calm mirror of the other — but each is also a parody of what it means to be human.[33]

Let us develop Blake's imagery a little further. There are several different means by which one may attempt to escape from the problems of the self that I have been discussing. One is the road often marked out by eighteenth-century empirical psychology, the road on which Cowper was traveling when he wrote:

'Tis woven in the world's great plan,
    And fix'd by heav'n's decree,
That all the true delights of man
    Should spring from *Sympathy*.
    . . . . . .
    Oh! grant, kind heav'n, to me,
Long as I draw ethereal air,
    Sweet Sensibility.[34]

This is the road that, followed far enough, leads to the realm of Har. But there is another road, one that leads away from the vale of sensibility; and that is the road Blake chose when he exalted the concept of independent, though potentially isolated, creative genius.

Har and Heva Bathing, Mnetha Looking On. Fitzwilliam Museum, Cambridge.

The particular lines that I have selected from Cowper may seem to indicate that the second road is in fact the way to creativity, but perhaps it is only the one likely to be chosen by writers who are more creative because they are more self-assured. This is impossible to decide; people on each path have created brilliant, and execrable, literature. Perhaps each road should be followed, if not with the blindness of Tiriel, then at least with a considerable degree of confidence in one's ideas. If one finds a basis for sustained artistic effort in any belief, however self-contradictory or logically impossible it may seem to others, then it is possible to say that he has chosen a "true" path. He may not even understand that he has chosen any particular "philosophy" or "psychological theory"; he may simply write fine literature. But if one sees too clearly the difficulties involved in choosing any of the paths available, he may, as Gray did, hesitate too long.

Here, like the Angel in *The Marriage of Heaven and Hell*, someone may cry, "Thy phantasy has imposed upon me & thou oughtest to be ashamed" (20; E 41, K 157). The conception of "two roads" is a fiction; it may be useful in analyzing a certain historical period, but even in that time the two roads did not exhaust men's options. Quite true: there are many options, and even Blake does not confine himself strictly to one "road." Wordsworth and Shelley are even better examples of authors who attempt to combine both solutions to problems of the self. And the particular problems that I have been discussing are not likely to arise unless one approaches the self in certain ways. If, for instance, one is not worried by the self's ability to conform to the outside world, troubled (conversely) by its tendency to isolation, or animated by a desire to find something unique or original in its responses to life, then one will probably have little use for any complex theories of "sympathy" or Blakean "Poetic Genius."

What I have said on these questions cannot be applied with ease to any literature other than that of the eighteenth and early nineteenth centuries. In our own century, the vocabulary of "genius" and "sensibility" has not worn well, and we have seen literary careers made on the premise that the old concepts of "self" and "society" are equally out of date — although some of our best writers

(Borges is a brilliant example) have occupied themselves with problems of the self that the eighteenth century would immediately recognize as its own. But modern political events, if nothing else, have put more pressure on the concepts of the individual self and its dignity than any such concepts can well bear. Contemporary literature often presents us either with social situations that seem to possess a barbaric life of their own, or with characters so isolated from effective contexts and effective selves that they can hardly be understood to be alive.

It is not clear, however, that scepticism about the self has a tendency to make the self any less important; the intellectual history of the eighteenth century indicates something just the opposite. The self may, perhaps, have vanished from the thoughts and writings of a few twentieth-century intellectuals, but their sentiments are conspicuously not shared by a majority of people in their audience, to whom self-analysis has given a set of beliefs, a ritual, and sometimes, no doubt, a source of real understanding.[35] It seems probable that modern adversities have merely rendered the quest for the self more complicated, more "desperate," and more exciting than it ever was before. A belief in the importance of those qualities that used to be called "genius" and "sensibility" has not disappeared from either modern life or modern literature; the words themselves have become outmoded, perhaps, because they have been overshadowed by that fascination with individual experience that initially helped to popularize them. Such words are felt to be too genteel to use in discussing the individual's difficult relations with the world, his need to comprehend his unconscious labyrinth of feelings, his desire to impose a unique structure on his life or work; they are outmoded, in short, because the problems involved in understanding the self's experience have grown more, not less, important to the modern mind. Much of modern literature is still engaged in attempts to determine the nature of a self that, like Gray's "pleasing anxious being," seems somehow more significant for its contradictions and ambiguities. Someday, such issues may lose all literary interest, but that event does not seem imminent.

Notes

Chapter 1
The Self as Stranger

1. *Conjectures on Original Composition* (1759; facs. rpt., Leeds: Scolar Press, 1966), pp. 52–53.

2. *The Complaint* [*Night Thoughts*], Night 6, in *The Works of the Author of the Night-Thoughts* (London, 1757), III, 157.

3. Edward Conze, trans., *Buddhist Scriptures* (Harmondsworth, Eng.: Penguin, 1959), p. 195. Conze provides an abstract of the debate as it appears in the fourth-century *Abhidharmakosha*.

4. For a general review of Locke's influence, see Kenneth MacLean, *John Locke and English Literature of the Eighteenth Century* (1936; rpt., New York: Russell and Russell, 1962).

5. For an account of Renaissance treatises on the self, see Paul A. Jorgensen, *Lear's Self-Discovery* (Berkeley: University of California Press, 1967), and Rolf Soellner, *Shakespeare's Patterns of Self-Knowledge* (Columbus: Ohio State University Press, 1972).

6. *There Is No Natural Religion,* in *The Poetry and Prose of William Blake,* ed. David V. Erdman (Garden City, N.Y.: Doubleday, 1970), p. 1.

7. *The Imagination as a Means of Grace: Locke and the Aesthetics of Romanticism* (Berkeley: University of California Press, 1960), p. 93. Tuveson's study of the moral and aesthetic theory of the eighteenth century analyzes a number of issues that are of considerable importance to my discussion of eighteenth-century concepts of self, including the problems of relativism and instability of the self that are inherent in empiricist ideas. Tuveson emphasizes the eighteenth century's attempt to base the dignity of the self on its possession of a moral sense and imagination. R. F. Brissenden's study of the sensibility movement — *Virtue in Distress: Studies in the Novel of Sentiment from Richardson to Sade* (New York: Barnes and Noble, 1974) — also offers a perceptive examination of the problems of subjectivism and relativism posed by empiricist assumptions about the mind. More recently, John O. Lyons has argued that the mid-eighteenth century was the period in which the idea of the "soul" began to be replaced by the modern concept of the "self"; see Lyons's informative and enter-

taining book *The Invention of the Self: The Hinge of Consciousness in the Eighteenth Century* (Carbondale: Southern Illinois University Press, 1978). Although Lyons does not attempt a systematic account of the origin of this concept, he discovers its effects in such diverse genres as biography, pornography, and travel literature; and he emphasizes the futility that often attended eighteenth- and nineteenth-century attempts to locate a "true self."

8. *A Common Sky: Philosophy and the Literary Imagination* (London: Chatto and Windus for Sussex University Press, 1974). W. B. Carnochan, *Confinement and Flight: An Essay on English Literature of the Eighteenth Century* (Berkeley: University of California Press, 1977), also views eighteenth-century images of psychic isolation as prophetic of modern preoccupations.

9. *The Concept of the Self in the French Enlightenment* (Geneva: Droz, 1969), pp. 74–75. Perkins's fine study shows (among other things) the complications that arose in French ideas about the self under the influence of British empiricism.

10. *Self-Knowledge and Self-Identity* (Ithaca: Cornell University Press, 1963), p. 40.

11. *Imagining a Self: Autobiography and Novel in Eighteenth-Century England* (Cambridge, Mass.: Harvard University Press, 1976). Spacks's concern with "the human need to declare not only the identity but the larger-than-life significance of the self" is related to my emphasis on these two issues, but her primary interest is in the ways in which one may suggest that the self "is both real and important" by shaping life into a literary pattern (pp. 18–19).

Chapter 2
Eighteenth–Century Philosophies of Self

1. *An Essay Concerning Human Understanding*, ed. Peter H. Nidditch (Oxford: Clarendon Press, 1975), bk. II, chap. xxvii, secs. 17, 9 (pp. 341, 335).

2. Ibid., bk. II, chap. i, secs. 1–5 (pp. 104–06); bk. II, chap. xxxii, sec. 14 (p. 388).

3. Ibid., bk. II, chap. viii (pp. 132–43).

4. Joseph Addison, *Spectator* No. 413 (June 24, 1712), in *The Spectator*, ed. Donald F. Bond (Oxford: Clarendon Press, 1965), III, 546–47.

5. *Night Thoughts*, Night 6, in *The Works of the Author of the Night-Thoughts* (London, 1757), III, 157–58.

6. *A Treatise of Human Nature*, ed. L. A. Selby-Bigge (Oxford: Clarendon Press, 1896), p. 67. This edition hereafter cited parenthetically as *Treatise*.

7. Review of *An Esssay on . . . Truth*, by James Beattie, *Critical Review*, 32 (1771), 454.

8. For a review of even earlier reactions to various kinds of "scepticism" implicit in Locke's philosophy, see John W. Yolton, *John Locke and the Way of Ideas* (Oxford: Clarendon Press, 1956).

9. Nuttall observes that "Shaftesbury is a true descendant of the Cambridge

Platonists as long as he successfully maintains his theory of disinterested morality . . . but turns empiricist as soon as he falls back upon the delighted analysis of psychological contents" — *A Common Sky: Philosophy and the Literary Imagination* (London: Chatto and Windus for Sussex University Press, 1974), p. 77n. On the nature and sources of Shaftesbury's philosophy, see Ernest Tuveson, "The Importance of Shaftesbury," *ELH*, 20 (1953), 267–99.

10. Anthony Ashley Cooper, Lord Shaftesbury, "The Moralists," pt. III, sec. i, in *Characteristicks of Men, Manners, Opinions, Times*, 4th ed. (London, 1727), II, 369.

11. "An Inquiry concerning Virtue, or Merit," bk. II, pt. ii, conclusion, in *Characteristicks*, II, 173.

12. "The Sceptic," in *Essays: Moral, Political and Literary* (London: Oxford University Press, 1963), p. 179.

13. "Miscellaneous Reflections," pt. IV, chap. i, in *Characteristicks*, III, 201.

14. Ibid., pp. 192–95.

15. *The Life, Unpublished Letters, and Philosophical Regimen of Anthony, Earl of Shaftesbury*, ed. Benjamin Rand (London: Sonnenschein, 1900), p. 136. In *Shaftesbury's Philosophy of Religion and Ethics: A Study in Enthusiasm* (Athens: Ohio University Press, 1967), Stanley Grean states that although Shaftesbury "is not consistent, and at times . . . means by 'self' whatever a person actually is at a given moment," the dominant meaning of "self" in his writings is the "true self" (p. 175).

16. "Soliloquy: Or, Advice to an Author," pt. I, sec. ii, in *Characteristicks*, I, 187.

17. "Inquiry concerning Virtue," bk. I, pt. iii, sec. 1, in *Characteristicks*, II, 43.

18. "Sensus Communis: An Essay on the Freedom of Wit and Humour," pt. III, sec. iii, in *Characteristicks*, I, 121. On the importance of social sensibility in Shaftesbury's philosophy, see Ernest Tuveson, "Shaftesbury and the Age of Sensibility," in *Studies in Criticism and Aesthetics, 1660–1800: Essays in Honor of Samuel Holt Monk*, ed. Howard Anderson and John S. Shea (Minneapolis: University of Minnesota Press, 1967), pp. 73–93.

19. *Sincerity and Authenticity* (Cambridge, Mass.: Harvard University Press, 1972), p. 5.

20. "Inquiry concerning Virtue," bk. II, pt. i, sec. 3, in *Characteristicks*, II, 95–97.

21. Henry Home, Lord Kames, *Essays on the Principles of Morality and Natural Religion* (Edinburgh, 1751), p. 231. Kames attributes this idea to Hume, but the context makes it clear that he is in fact adopting — and subtly altering — one of Hume's ideas so that he can use it in support of his own theories.

22. Ibid., p. 240. Kames attempts to steer between the two extremes by arguing that an "original" perception of self "accompanies" one's external impressions but arises from an "internal sense" (pp. 231–36).

23. *An Essay on the Nature and Immutability of Truth, in Opposition to Sophistry and Scepticism*, rev. ed., in *Essays on . . . Truth, . . . On Poetry and Music . . .* (Dublin, 1778), I, 69.

24. Ibid., p. 213.

25. *An Inquiry into the Human Mind, on the Principles of Common Sense,* 7th ed. (Edinburgh, 1814), p. v.

26. Ibid., chap. I, sec. i (pp. 2–3).

27. *Essay on . . . Truth,* in *Essays,* I, 199.

28. *Virtue in Distress: Studies in the Novel of Sentiment from Richardson to Sade* (New York: Barnes and Noble, 1974), p. 54.

29. Joseph Butler, "Of the Nature of Virtue," in *The Analogy of Religion, Natural and Revealed, to the Constitution and Course of Nature,* 2nd ed. (London, 1736), pp. 451–67.

30. Hutcheson sets forth his theories in *An Inquiry into the Original of Our Ideas of Beauty and Virtue* (London, 1725), *An Essay on the Nature and Conduct of the Passions and Affections* (London, 1728), and *A System of Moral Philosophy,* 2 vols. (London, 1755). In *The Imagination as a Means of Grace: Locke and the Aesthetics of Romanticism* (Berkeley: University of California Press, 1960), Tuveson provides a detailed examination of the concept of autonomous inner senses as a source of spiritual value and considers the problem of subjectivity associated with this concept; for a summary of his views, see esp. pp. 164–65.

31. *Night Thoughts,* Night 8, in *Works,* III, 258. This is the true self, but Young emphasizes the fact that it has strong competition from another self, which is actually "fond of ev'ry vice."

32. *An Examination of Dr. Reid's Inquiry . . .* (London, 1774), p. 121.

33. *Inquiry into the Human Mind,* chap. I, sec. ii (pp. 5–6).

34. Annotations to Reynolds, in *The Poetry and Prose of William Blake,* ed. David V. Erdman (Garden City, N.Y.: Doubleday, 1970), p. 645.

35. Stanley Grean reviews this very slippery issue in *Shaftesbury's Philosophy,* pp. 43, 204–07.

36. Even Hutcheson, *Inquiry into . . . Beauty and Virtue,* 2nd ed. (London, 1726), p. xvi, maintains that the *"moral Sense* has no relation to innate Ideas."

37. "Suggestions toward a Genealogy of the 'Man of Feeling,'" *ELH,* 1 (1934), 205–30.

38. "Latitudinarianism and Sensibility: The Genealogy of the 'Man of Feeling' Reconsidered," *Modern Philology,* 75 (1977), 159–83.

39. "Nerves, Spirits, and Fibres: Towards Defining the Origins of Sensibility," in *Studies in the Eighteenth Century III,* ed. R. F. Brissenden and J. C. Eade (Toronto: University of Toronto Press, 1976), pp. 137–57.

40. On this issue, see G. S. Rousseau, "Science and the Discovery of the Imagination in Enlightened England," *Eighteenth-Century Studies,* 3 (1969), 108–35; and Brissenden, *Virtue in Distress,* pp. 20–21, 30–49.

41. *Critical Review,* 9 (1760), 38–39.

42. "Inquiry concerning Virtue," bk. II, pt. ii, sec. 1, in *Characteristicks,* II, 99.

43. *A System of Moral Philosophy,* I, 19–21.

44. *A Treatise on Virtue and Happiness,* 2nd ed. (London, 1736), pp. 134, 146.

45. *Passion and Value in Hume's "Treatise"* (Edinburgh: Edinburgh University Press, 1966), p. 45. For another defense of Hume, see Philip Mercer, *Sympathy and Ethics* (Oxford: Clarendon Press, 1972), pp. 27–30. Yet Mercer's contention that Hume attempts to "vindicate the common-sense belief in personal identity" would have surprised Hume's contemporaries.

46. *Critical Review,* 7 (1759), 384–86.

47. *Monthly Review,* 21 (1759), 2. For attribution to Rose, see Benjamin Christie Nangle, *"The Monthly Review," First Series 1749–1789: Indexes of Contributors and Articles* (Oxford: Clarendon Press, 1934), p. 199.

48. *Annual Register* (1759), p. 485. For attribution to Burke, see Thomas Wellsted Copeland, "Edmund Burke and the Book Reviews in Dodsley's *Annual Register,*" *PMLA,* 57 (1942), 446–68.

49. *The Theory of Moral Sentiments,* ed. D. D. Raphael and A. L. Macfie (Oxford: Clarendon Press, 1976), p. 9. This edition, based on the 6th ed. of 1790, is hereafter cited parenthetically as *TMS.*

50. See, for instance, James Bonar, *Moral Sense* (New York: Macmillan, 1930), pp. 192–95; and D. D. Raphael, "The Impartial Spectator," in *Essays on Adam Smith,* ed. Andrew S. Skinner and Thomas Wilson (Oxford: Clarendon Press, 1975), pp. 83–99.

51. This can be exaggerated, as in Max Scheler's vulgarization of Smith's theory: "According to Adam Smith, a man unjustly condemned and universally considered to be guilty should also acknowledge his guilt himself"—*The Nature of Sympathy,* trans. Peter Heath (London: Routledge, 1954), p. 6.

52. *Adam Smith's Science of Morals* (London: Allen and Unwin, 1971), pp. 127–39. See also Campbell, "Scientific Explanation and Ethical Justification in the *Moral Sentiments,*" in *Essays on Adam Smith,* ed. Skinner and Wilson, pp. 68–82.

53. As Brissenden suggests in *Virtue in Distress,* esp. pp. 53–55. In commenting on the works of Smith and others, Brissenden gives more emphasis than I might to the role of reason in sentimentalist ideas; but he correctly characterizes sympathy and sensibility as concepts expressive of both empiricism and idealism, concepts that could be used to describe "feeling" as individual and subjective, on the one hand, and yet, on the other, as "reasonable," authoritative, and much inclined to the social virtues.

54. David Hartley, *Observations on Man, His Frame, His Duty, and His Expectations,* 2 vols. (London, 1749). On self-annihilation, see esp. pt. II, props. 67, 68 (II, 280–90).

55. *Sincerity and Authenticity,* p. 54.

Chapter 3
Self and the Aesthetics of Sensibility

1. *Ode on the Poetical Character,* ll. 55–60, in *Gray and Collins: Poetical Works,* ed. Austin Lane Poole, 3rd ed. (London: Oxford University Press, 1937). Subsequent quotations from Collins are from this edition.

2. "Mother, Memory, Muse and Poetry after Pope," *ELH*, 44 (1977), 312–36.

3. "Structure and Substantiality in Later Eighteenth-Century Literature," *Studies in Burke and His Time*, 15 (Winter 1973–74), 143–54.

4. *Conjectures on Original Composition* (1759; facs. rpt., Leeds: Scolar Press, 1966), pp. 26–27, 53.

5. Ibid., pp. 42, 35.

6. *An Essay on Original Genius; and Its Various Modes of Exertion* . . . (London, 1767), p. 5.

7. *An Essay on Genius* (1774; facs. rpt., New York: Garland Publishing, 1970), p. 3.

8. Ibid., pp. 3–4, 215–18.

9. *Critical Observations on the Writings of the Most Celebrated Original Geniuses in Poetry* (1770; facs. rpt., New York: Garland Publishing, 1971), p. 341.

10. Ibid., pp. 353, 80.

11. *Essay on Original Genius*, pp. 152–54.

12. *Critical Observations*, pp. 74–76.

13. *A Dissertation upon Genius* . . . , ed. William Bruce Johnson (1755; facs. rpt., Delmar, N.Y.: Scholars' Facsimiles, 1973), passim.

14. *An Essay on Taste* (London, 1759), pp. 173–74.

15. *From Classic to Romantic: Premises of Taste in Eighteenth-Century England* (Cambridge, Mass.: Harvard University Press, 1946), esp. pp. 93–159.

16. *Critical Review*, 38 (1774), 329.

17. *The Imagination as a Means of Grace: Locke and the Aesthetics of Romanticism* (Berkeley: University of California Press, 1960), p. 150. On the association of genius with passive sensibility, see also pp. 90, 136, 148–55.

18. *Essay on Taste*, p. 178n.

19. *Essay on Genius*, pp. 407, 367–69.

20. William Wordsworth, Preface to *Lyrical Ballads*, in *Literary Criticism of William Wordsworth*, ed. Paul M. Zall (Lincoln: University of Nebraska Press, 1966), p. 43.

21. *Essays on the Principles of Morality and Natural Religion* (Edinburgh, 1751), pp. 24, 17; *Elements of Criticism* (1762; facs. rpt., New York: Johnson Reprints Corp., 1967), I, iii, 13. For another pronouncement on sympathetic self-approbation, see Hugh Blair, *Lectures on Rhetoric and Belles Lettres*, ed. Harold F. Harding (1783; facs. rpt., Carbondale: Southern Illinois University Press, 1965), II, 495–96.

22. *Elements*, II, 151–52. Cf. Blair, *Lectures*, I, 364–65, II, 507–08; Bate, *Classic to Romantic*, pp. 142–43.

23. Laurence Sterne, *A Sentimental Journey through France and Italy by Mr. Yorick*, ed. Gardner D. Stout, Jr. (Berkeley: University of California Press, 1967), pp. 277–78.

24. *Sympathy; Or, a Sketch of the Social Passions. A Poem* (London, 1781), pp. 45–46.

25. William Cowper, "To Miss ——," ll. 29–30, in *Poetical Works*, ed. H. S. Milford, 4th ed., corrected by Norma Russell (London: Oxford University Press, 1971), p. 286.

26. Thomas Gray, *De Principiis Cogitandi*, ll. 32–63, as translated in *The Complete Poems of Thomas Gray*, ed. H. W. Starr and J. R. Hendrickson (Oxford: Clarendon Press, 1966), pp. 163–64; Cowper, *Table Talk*, ll. 486–87, in *Poetical Works*, p. 11; William Blake, *The Four Zoas*, p. 11, l. 15, in *The Poetry and Prose of William Blake*, ed. David V. Erdman (Garden City, N.Y.: Doubleday, 1970), p. 302.

27. "The Enthusiast. An Ode," in *Poems on Several Occasions, with the Roman Father, a Tragedy* (London, 1754), pp. 87–91.

28. *Critical Observations*, pp. 350, 352–53.

29. Samuel Johnson, *The History of Rasselas Prince of Abissinia*, ed. Geoffrey Tillotson and Brian Jenkins (London: Oxford University Press, 1971), chap. XLV (p. 119). John A. Dussinger, considering Goldsmith's *Vicar of Wakefield*, has also discussed sensibility's potential for isolating the self within its own narcissism; see *The Discourse of the Mind in Eighteenth-Century Fiction* (The Hague: Mouton, 1974), pp. 148–72.

30. *Critical Observations*, pp. 339–40.

31. *The Mirror*, Nos. 99 and 100 (Apr. 18 and 22, 1780), in *The Works of Henry Mackenzie, Esq.* (Edinburgh, 1808), IV, 375, 392, 376.

32. *A Course of Lectures on Oratory and Criticism* (1777; facs. rpt., New York: Garland Publishing, 1971), pp. 126–27, 147.

33. Ibid., pp. 146–47, 127–28.

34. Monk, *The Sublime: A Study in Critical Theories in XVIII-Century England* (1935; rpt., Ann Arbor: University of Michigan Press, 1960); Nicolson, *Mountain Gloom and Mountain Glory: The Development of the Aesthetics of the Infinite* (Ithaca: Cornell University Press, 1959).

35. *Night Thoughts*, Night 9, in *The Works of the Author of the Night-Thoughts* (London, 1757), IV, 37.

36. Ibid., pp. 39, 37.

37. See, for example, Thomas Nettleton, *A Treatise on Virtue and Happiness*, 2nd ed. (London, 1736), pp. 146–47; Gerard, *Essay on Taste*, pp. 74–75; Kames, *Elements*, I, 73–75; Blair, *Lectures*, II, 478–80.

38. *Adam Smith's Science of Morals* (London: Allen and Unwin, 1971), p. 65. See also A. L. Macfie, *The Individual in Society: Papers on Adam Smith* (London: Allen and Unwin, 1967), pp. 49–50.

39. *An Essay on Poetry and Music, as They Affect the Mind*, in *Essays on . . . Truth, . . . On Poetry and Music* (Dublin, 1778), II, 170–75.

40. James Boswell, *Boswell's Life of Johnson*, ed. George Birkbeck Hill, rev. L. F. Powell, II (Oxford: Clarendon Press, 1934), 94.

41. *Rambler* No. 60 (Oct. 13, 1750), in *The Rambler*, ed. W. J. Bate and Albrecht B. Strauss (New Haven: Yale University Press, 1969), I, 318–19. Johnson's views on

sympathy are exhaustively studied in John B. Radner's valuable article, "Samuel Johnson, the Deceptive Imagination, and Sympathy," *Studies in Burke and His Time*, 16 (1974), 23–46.

42. Blair, *Lectures*, II, 502–05. Gordon McKenzie, *Critical Responsiveness: A Study of the Psychological Current in Later Eighteenth-Century Criticism*, University of California Publications in English, 20 (Berkeley: University of California Press, 1949), esp. pp. 210–14, provides numerous examples of critical insistence on the emotional effectiveness of familiar material.

43. "Some Remarks on Eighteenth-Century 'Delicacy,' with a Note on Hugh Kelly's *False Delicacy* (1768)," *Journal of English and Germanic Philology*, 61 (1962), 1–4.

44. *Samuel Richardson: Dramatic Novelist* (London: Methuen, 1973), pp. 477–80.

45. *A Critical Dissertation on the Poems of Ossian*, in *The Works of Ossian, the Son of Fingal*, by James Macpherson, 3rd ed. (London, 1765), II, 346, 381.

46. Ibid., pp. 396, 332–33. Cf. Louis I. Bredvold, *The Natural History of Sensibility* (Detroit: Wayne State University Press, 1962), p. 66: "As virtue and genius were both excellences of human nature, they seemed to the eighteenth century to be closely related, and in men of great endowment almost one and the same."

47. *Critical Dissertation*, in *Works of Ossian*, II, 436, 390.

48. *Virtue in Distress: Studies in the Novel of Sentiment from Richardson to Sade* (New York: Barnes and Noble, 1974), p. 22.

49. *Essay on Genius*, pp. 102–03.

50. "Essay, Supplementary to the Preface," in *Literary Criticism*, p. 182.

51. *Elements*, III, 365. Cf. Smith, *The Theory of Moral Sentiments*, ed. D. D. Raphael and A. L. Macfie (Oxford: Clarendon Press, 1976), pp. 200–11, on principles of morals; Gerard, *Essay on Taste*, pp. 77–78, on principles of taste.

52. See Edward Niles Hooker, "The Discussion of Taste, from 1750 to 1770, and the New Trends in Literary Criticism," *PMLA*, 49 (1934), 577–92.

53. "Towards Defining an Age of Sensibility," *ELH*, 23 (1956), 144–52.

54. *To the Palace of Wisdom: Studies in Order and Energy from Dryden to Blake* (Garden City, N.Y.: Doubleday, 1964), p. 375.

55. Preface to *Lyrical Ballads*, in *Literary Criticism*, pp. 48–49.

Chapter 4
Defining the Self: Samuel Richardson's Clarissa

1. *Clarissa: Or, The History of a Young Lady* (London: Everyman's Library-Dent, 1932), I, 201; Shakespeare Head Edition (Oxford: Basil Blackwell, 1930), I, 295. All quotations are drawn from the Everyman edition; page numbers for each edition are cited parenthetically in the text as EL and SH respectively.

2. *The Early Masters of English Fiction* (Lawrence: University of Kansas Press, 1956), pp. 74–75.

3. "Clarissa Harlowe and Her Times," *Essays in Criticism*, 5 (1955), 328. Al-

though I cannot agree with all of Hill's conclusions, his essay (pp. 315–40), together with Ian Watt's *The Rise of the Novel: Studies in Defoe, Richardson and Fielding* (Berkeley: University of California Press, 1957), must be considered in any attempt to place *Clarissa* in the context of the increasing economic, philosophical, and religious "individualism" of the eighteenth century. Leo Braudy has contrasted Richardson's conception of the assertive self with the self overpowered by God which forms the general theme of Puritan spiritual autobiography; see Braudy's essay "Penetration and Impenetrability in *Clarissa*," in *New Approaches to Eighteenth-Century Literature: Selected Papers from the English Institute*, ed. Phillip Harth (New York: Columbia University Press, 1974), p. 180n. The essay (pp. 177–206) provides an interesting study of Clarissa's attempt to protect and assert a "pure" identity based on inner principle.

4. *The Self Observed: Swift, Johnson, Wordsworth* (Baltimore: Johns Hopkins Press, 1972), pp. 10, 29. Golden also remarks the important fact that the "awareness of division . . . stimulated the attempts in the eighteenth century to seek those elements of identity which can help the self . . . to tie the outer to the inner through sympathetic communication" (p. 29).

5. Shaftesbury, "Soliloquy: Or, Advice to an Author," pt. I, secs. i and ii, in *Characteristicks of Men, Manners, Opinions, Times*, 4th ed. (London, 1727), I, 153–76; Smith, *The Theory of Moral Sentiments*, ed. D. D. Raphael and A. L. Macfie (Oxford: Clarendon Press, 1976), p. 113.

6. On the place of Clarissa's moral individualism in the eighteenth-century sentimentalist tradition, see R. F. Brissenden, *Virtue in Distress: Studies in the Novel of Sentiment from Richardson to Sade* (New York: Barnes and Noble, 1974), esp. pp. 24–26; on *Clarissa's* place in the context of seventeenth- and eighteenth-century empirical investigations of the self, see G. S. Rousseau, "Nerves, Spirits, and Fibres: Towards Defining the Origins of Sensibility," in *Studies in the Eighteenth Century III*, ed. R. F. Brissenden and J. C. Eade (Toronto: University of Toronto Press, 1976), pp. 137–57.

7. H. G. Ward noted that Richardson shows his familiarity with Locke's *Some Thoughts concerning Education* in the sequel to *Pamela* but concluded that he had not read Locke's *Essay* because the word "idea" does not occur in his novels — "Samuel Richardson and the English Philosophers," *Notes and Queries*, 11th ser., 3 (1911), 5–6.

8. "Conscience and the Pattern of Christian Perfection in *Clarissa*," *PMLA*, 81 (1966), 236–45.

9. *An Essay on the Nature and Conduct of the Passions and Affections* (London, 1728), pp. 4–7.

10. *Virtue in Distress*, pp. 34–35, 159–86.

11. This issue is also discussed by Steven M. Cohan, "*Clarissa* and the Individuation of Character," *ELH*, 43 (1976), 163–83.

12. See Patricia Meyer Spacks, *Imagining a Self: Autobiography and Novel in Eighteenth-Century England* (Cambridge, Mass.: Harvard University Press, 1976),

pp. 208–18, for an interesting consideration of the question of audience approval in Richardson's *Pamela*. Morris Golden, *Richardson's Characters* (Ann Arbor: University of Michigan Press, 1963), pp. 144–81, discusses "the peculiar need for an audience by most characters in most actions" in all of Richardson's novels (p. 159).

13. *Samuel Richardson and the Eighteenth-Century Puritan Character* (Hamden, Conn.: Archon Books – Shoe String Press, 1972); see esp. pp. 2–3. In discussing Clarissa's need to define herself in a stable moral and social order, especially that of her family, I am generally in agreement with Wolff's argument; I also support her conclusion that Clarissa's death-wish can be attributed, at least in part, to her inability to identify herself in that way (pp. 156–57). But I believe that the eighteenth-century concepts of sympathy and sensibility may explain much about the novel that the "Puritan" tradition, however broadly defined, cannot. Cohan, "*Clarissa* and the Individuation of Character," describes Clarissa as relying on social roles in an attempt to stabilize her sense of self, and argues that the only role through which she can assert herself is that of a "self-conscious martyr." He is not concerned, however, with the conflict between her innate "true self" and her need for social sympathy.

14. Anthony Winner, "Richardson's Lovelace: Character and Prediction," *Texas Studies in Literature and Language*, 14 (1972), 53–75, considers Lovelace "a demonic version of the man of feeling," "a flux of passionate feeling" who cannot define himself except by means of sensation and external challenges but lacks an appropriate field of action in his "pacific age and society." On Lovelace's frustrated abilities, see also John Carroll, "Lovelace as Tragic Hero," *University of Toronto Quarterly*, 42 (1972), 14–25.

15. Mark Kinkead-Weekes, *Samuel Richardson: Dramatic Novelist* (London: Methuen, 1973), also discusses the conflict between a self capable of true feeling and a rakish identity required by Lovelace's need for superiority; see esp. pp. 150–57, 186–87.

16. T. C. Duncan Eaves and Ben D. Kimpel, analyzing Lovelace's need to maintain his false superiority and his image before other people, remark that he is an example of the fact that "there are conventions for rakes at least as rigid as the conventions of virtue" – *Samuel Richardson: A Biography* (Oxford: Clarendon Press, 1971), p. 266.

17. Kinkead-Weekes, *Richardson: Dramatic Novelist*, p. 273, writes that Lovelace's "agon" is a "death struggle between two possible selves" – an "inner" self and a rakish one. If so, the struggle results, even before his literal death, in the symbolic death of both selves.

18. *Imagining a Self*, p. 20.

19. Norman Rabkin, "*Clarissa*: A Study in the Nature of Convention," *ELH*, 23 (1956), 207, states that Clarissa puts "abstract social obligation" before "knowledge of moral right"; and she is frequently capable of doing so. I cannot agree with Rabkin, however, when he equates "convention" with her "soul" (p. 206 and pp. 204–17 passim). The aspect of Clarissa's self that Richardson most emphasizes is her moral individualism.

20. Kinkead-Weekes, *Richardson: Dramatic Novelist*, p. 169, notes that here Clarissa is, perhaps, displaying her "pride" even as she denounces it. This is certainly true; but Clarissa does not recognize that she is doing so, and Richardson, in sympathy with his character, perhaps does not either.

21. See Allan Wendt, "Clarissa's Coffin," *Philological Quarterly*, 39 (1960), 489.

22. Golden, *Richardson's Characters*, p. 145, notes that in general Richardson's virtuous characters "want to be set firmly in the[ir] surrounding groups, because of the security and the approval that such a setting involves. Even the bold bad young men need a small circle of friends before whom to shine, defiant though they may be of the judgment of the world at large."

23. *The Genealogy of Morals*, Second Essay, sec. VII, in *The Birth of Tragedy and The Genealogy of Morals*, trans. Francis Golffing (Garden City, N.Y.: Doubleday, 1956), p. 200.

24. *Literary Essays* (New York: Philosophical Library, 1957), p. 28. Braudy, "Penetration and Impenetrability," pp. 192, 199, stresses the fact that Clarissa seeks to define herself as independent of other people while at the same time seeking to be approved by them as an exemplar.

25. *Johnsonian Miscellanies*, ed. George Birkbeck Hill (Oxford: Clarendon Press, 1897), I, 282.

Chapter 5
Contexts of Significance: Thomas Gray

1. *The Task*, VI, 940–43, in *Poetical Works*, ed. H. S. Milford, 4th ed., corrected by Norma Russell (London: Oxford University Press, 1971), pp. 239–40.

2. *The Lives of the Most Eminent English Poets* (London, 1781), IV, 485.

3. Lines 89–92. All quotations from Gray's poetry are from *The Complete Poems of Thomas Gray*, ed. H. W. Starr and J. R. Hendrickson (Oxford: Clarendon Press, 1966).

4. Gray to Horace Walpole, Jan. or Feb. 1748, *Correspondence of Thomas Gray*, ed. Paget Toynbee and Leonard Whibley, corrections and additions by H. W. Starr (Oxford: Clarendon Press, 1971), I, 302.

5. Norton Nicholls, "Reminiscences of Gray," in *Correspondence*, III, 1289. See also Gray to Beattie, July 2, 1770, ibid., p. 1141.

6. On the decline of faith see Gray to Richard Stonhewer, Aug. 18, 1758, ibid., II, 583. The best survey of Gray's intellectual interests is William Powell Jones, *Thomas Gray, Scholar* (1937; rpt., New York: Russell and Russell, 1965).

7. See, for example, Gray to Nicholls, Sept. 23, 1766, *Correspondence*, III, 935–36; Gray's lines for an epitaph on Mrs. William Mason, *Complete Poems*, p. 105.

8. The epitaph seems to have been written for Robin Wharton; it appears in *Complete Poems*, p. 104.

9. The essay is contained in William Mason's *Memoirs* of Gray, pp. 265–68, in

The Poems of Mr. Gray. To Which Are Prefixed Memoirs of His Life and Writings (York, 1775).

10. Alexander Pope, *An Essay on Man*, Twickenham Ed., ed. Maynard Mack (London: Methuen, 1950), I.17–18 (p. 14).

11. See "Fragments or Minutes of Essays," in *The Works of the Late Right Honorable Henry St. John, Lord Viscount Bolingbroke* (London, 1754), V, 372–92, on Wollaston, *The Religion of Nature Delineated*, 4th ed. (London, 1726), p. 209. Bolingbroke's religious ideas are stated at large in the essays composing vol. V of his *Works*.

12. "Reminiscences," in *Correspondence*, III, 1289.

13. On the eighteenth-century Lockean approach to this issue, see Kenneth MacLean, *John Locke and English Literature of the Eighteenth Century* (1936; rpt., New York: Russell and Russell, 1962), pp. 146 ff.

14. "Those—Dying Then," in *The Poems of Emily Dickinson*, ed. Thomas H. Johnson (Cambridge, Mass.: Harvard University Press, 1955), III, 1069.

15. Two interesting discussions of this issue are: G. S. Rousseau, "Gray's *Elegy* Reconsidered," *The Spectator*, Oct. 2, 1971, p. 490; and Jean H. Hagstrum, "Gray's Sensibility," in *Fearful Joy: Papers from the Thomas Gray Bicentenary Conference at Carleton University*, ed. James Downey and Ben Jones (Montreal: McGill-Queen's University Press, 1974), pp. 6–19.

16. Roger Martin, Gray's perceptive biographer, examines his "impression de néant" and provides additional examples of it in his *Essai sur Thomas Gray* (Paris: Presses Universitaires de France, 1934), pp. 22–23.

17. Jan. 14, 1735, *Correspondence*, I, 18.

18. Mar. 28, 1738, and Dec., 1734, ibid., pp. 83–84, 12.

19. April 12, 1770, ibid., III, 1118.

20. Quoted in Mason, *Memoirs*, pp. 202–03.

21. Sept. 11, 1746, *Correspondence*, I, 240.

22. "Blake on Gray: Outlines of Recognition," in *Fearful Joy*, p. 129.

23. To Walpole, Feb. 3, 1746, *Correspondence*, I, 230.

24. I am in general agreement with Roger Lonsdale's conclusions, in his insightful discussion of the poems of 1742, about the sterility of isolated self-consciousness; see "The Poetry of Thomas Gray: Versions of the Self," *Proceedings of the British Academy*, 59 (1973), 114–18.

25. Among the critics who have applauded Gray's original conclusion are: R. W. Ketton-Cremer, *Thomas Gray: A Biography* (Cambridge: Cambridge University Press, 1955), pp. 98–100; F. W. Bateson, *English Poetry: A Critical Introduction*, 2nd ed., rev. (New York: Barnes and Noble, 1966), pp. 128–31; and Clarence Tracy, "'Melancholy Mark'd Him for Her Own': Thomas Gray Two Hundred Years Afterwards," *Transactions of the Royal Society of Canada*, 4th ser., 9 (1971), 318.

26. Lonsdale, "Poetry of Thomas Gray," pp. 107–08, furnishes additional reasons for regarding "the attempted calm of this conclusion to the poem" as "precarious."

George T. Wright, in "Stillness and the Argument of Gray's *Elegy*," *Modern Philology*, 74 (1977), 381–89, emphasizes the negative implications of the churchyard's stillness and accordingly finds the resignation of Gray's first conclusion inconsistent with the poem's argument. But although Wright may be correct in suggesting that "stillness and resistance to it compose [Gray's] argument," I cannot agree with his statement that the *Elegy*'s real "point" is "that we all need epitaphs" (p. 387); nor can I agree that, in the context of the poem, epitaphs and a reliance on God provide a real fulfillment of man's desire to resist death.

27. Jack, "Gray's *Elegy* Reconsidered," in *From Sensibility to Romanticism: Essays Presented to Frederick A. Pottle*, ed. Frederick W. Hilles and Harold Bloom (New York: Oxford University Press, 1965), p. 146.

28. Nov. 1747, *Correspondence*, I, 289.

29. Mar. 9, 1755, ibid., p. 420.

30. Most of the critics who have engaged in the long debate about whether the *Elegy*'s description of the speaker refers personally to Gray or is purely impersonal or conventional would agree with Ketton-Cremer's judgment that the Swain offers a "strangely dramatised description of a poet in aspect and behaviour the complete antithesis of Gray" (*Thomas Gray*, p. 101). Such assertions seem rather surprising in view of what we know of Gray's character; they are well refuted by Hagstrum in "Gray's Sensibility," pp. 16–17.

31. Frank Brady, "Structure and Meaning in Gray's *Elegy*," in *From Sensibility to Romanticism*, pp. 185–87, gives more emphasis than I would to the speaker's partial fulfillment of himself through his one friendship, but he correctly emphasizes the speaker's isolation and the fact that the Epitaph shows that "only the individual can know to what extent he has fulfilled himself."

32. Norton Nicholls wrote, "I asked him how he felt when he composed the *Bard*. 'Why I felt myself the bard.'" See "Reminiscences," *Correspondence*, III, 1290.

33. "The Proper Language of Poetry: Gray, Johnson, and Others," in *Fearful Joy*, pp. 92–93.

34. *The History of Rasselas Prince of Abissinia*, ed. Geoffrey Tillotson and Brian Jenkins (London: Oxford University Press, 1971), chap. XLIV (p. 114).

35. Morris Golden, *Thomas Gray* (New York: Twayne, 1964), pp. 111, 113, comments on the way in which Gray "catches and amplifies . . . the sense of elemental amorality of the divinities" in *The Fatal Sisters*.

36. Gray's text is translated in *Complete Poems*, pp. 216–18.

37. As quoted in *Complete Poems*, p. 234.

38. Mason quotes and discusses the Commonplace Book entry in *Poems of Mr. Gray*, pp. 91–92.

39. "The Cistern and the Fountain: Art and Reality in Pope and Gray," in *Studies in Criticism and Aesthetics*, ed. Howard Anderson and John S. Shea (Minneapolis: University of Minnesota Press, 1967), pp. 174–75.

40. See Jean Hagstrum, *The Sister Arts: The Tradition of Literary Pictorialism*

and English Poetry from Dryden to Gray (Chicago: University of Chicago Press, 1958), pp. 301–14; and Patricia Meyer Spacks, *The Poetry of Vision: Five Eighteenth-Century Poets* (Cambridge, Mass.: Harvard University Press, 1967), pp. 110–18.

Chapter 6
Self and Persona: Thomas Chatterton

1. *The Complete Works of Thomas Chatterton*, ed. Donald S. Taylor and Benjamin B. Hoover (Oxford: Clarendon Press, 1971), I, 341. All quotations from Chatterton are from this edition, hereafter cited as *Works*. I have relied on Taylor's datings of Chatterton's works and on Taylor's translations of the Rowleyan language in those cases in which Chatterton has not supplied his own translations. Taylor's new book, *Thomas Chatterton's Art: Experiments in Imagined History* (Princeton: Princeton University Press, 1978), provides an illuminating analysis of Chatterton's artistic development.

2. *A Life of Thomas Chatterton* (New York: Scribner, 1930), p. 271. See also Bertrand H. Bronson, "Thomas Chatterton," in *The Age of Johnson: Essays Presented to Chauncey Brewster Tinker*, ed. Frederick W. Hilles (New Haven: Yale University Press, 1949), p. 251. Bronson's essay remains one of the most perceptive discussions of Chatterton's psychology.

3. Norton Nicholls, "Reminiscences of Gray," in *Correspondence of Thomas Gray*, ed. Paget Toynbee and Leonard Whibley, corrections and additions by H. W. Starr (Oxford: Clarendon Press, 1971), III, 1290.

4. To William Barrett, Feb. or Mar. 1770, *Works*, I, 494.

5. Alexander Pope, *An Essay on Criticism*, ll. 84–87, in *Pastoral Poetry and An Essay on Criticism*, Twickenham Ed., ed. E. Audra and Aubrey Williams (London: Methuen, 1961), pp. 248–49.

6. Taylor, *Chatterton's Art*, p. 191, also points out Rowley's apparent indebtedness to Pope.

7. *Conjectures on Original Composition* (1759; facs. rpt., Leeds: Scolar Press, 1966), pp. 30–31.

8. *Life*, pp. 333–34.

9. In "Journal 6th," for example: "Opinion is the only guide / By which our Senses are supply'd" (ll. 5–6; *Works*, I, 365). In "Happiness," Chatterton first disparages the vagaries of religious conscience but concludes by advising: "Then Friend let Inclination be thy Guide" (l. 143; *Works*, I, 408). It is difficult to determine the extent and nature of Chatterton's "freethinking," but it seems to have been something more extreme than Georges Lamoine considers it in his essay on "La Pensée religieuse et le suicide de Thomas Chatterton," *Etudes Anglaises*, 23 (1970), 369–79.

10. It is perhaps some indication of the fluid nature of history that the suicide, the best-known episode of Chatterton's life, has lately been called into question.

Richard Holmes, a sensitive interpreter of the poet's life and works, has assembled evidence that suggests that his death may have resulted from an accidental overdose of venereal remedies, and so eminent a Chattertonian as Donald S. Taylor has found this evidence worthy of consideration: see Holmes, "Thomas Chatterton: The Case Re-opened," *Cornhill*, 178 (1970), 203–51; Taylor, *Chatterton's Art*, pp. 4, 155–56, 313, 328.

11. *Conjectures*, p. 15.

12. "The Historical Sense of Thomas Chatterton," *ELH*, 11 (1944), 117–34.

13. On the general problem of originality faced by both Chatterton and Macpherson, see Robert Folkenflik, "Macpherson, Chatterton, Blake and the Great Age of Literary Forgery," *Centennial Review*, 18 (1974), 378–91. Although Folkenflik's emphasis differs significantly from mine, his essay provides a valuable discussion of the late-eighteenth-century concern with original genius and its relation to the works of both poets.

14. *The Works of Ossian, the Son of Fingal*, by James Macpherson, 3rd ed. (London, 1765), I, 283.

15. *Critical Dissertation*, ibid., II, 338.

16. Ibid., pp. 340–41. C. S. Lewis, "Addison," in *Eighteenth-Century English Literature: Modern Essays in Criticism*, ed. James L. Clifford (New York: Oxford University Press, 1959), pp. 154–55, characterizes Rowley and Ossian as "wish-fulfilments" of eighteenth-century conceptions of what medieval genius should have been.

17. Cf. Taylor's note on Chatterton's "mixed feelings" about Ossianic poetry: *Works*, II, 949–50.

18. On the importance of the quest for heroes in the Rowley poems, see also Taylor's discussion (*Chatterton's Art*, pp. 79ff.) of Chatterton's two types of heroic figures — the warriors and rulers who are traditional protagonists of heroic literature, and the bourgeois heroes with whose lives Chatterton might more easily identify his own.

19. See Bronson, "Thomas Chatterton," pp. 243–44; Meyerstein, *Life*, p. 217.

20. My account of the psychology of Chatterton's play generally follows that of Irvin B. Kroese in "Chatterton's *Aella* and Chatterton," *Studies in English Literature, 1500-1900*, 12 (1972), 557–66.

21. "Chatterton's *Aella*," p. 564.

22. *An Essay on Original Genius; and Its Various Modes of Exertion* . . . (London, 1767), pp. 152–53, 135–38. As Donald S. Taylor has reminded me, Chatterton shows a knowledge of Duff in "Memoirs of a Sad Dog," *Works*, I, 655.

23. "Historical Sense of Thomas Chatterton," pp. 123–24.

24. *A Specimen of a Commentary on Shakspeare* (1794), ed. Alan Over and Mary Bell (London: Methuen, 1967), p. 190.

25. Annotations to Wordsworth's *Poems*, in *The Poetry and Prose of William Blake*, ed. David V. Erdman (Garden City, N.Y.: Doubleday, 1970), p. 655.

Chapter 7
Self and Perception: William Cowper

1. Percy Bysshe Shelley, *A Defence of Poetry*, in *Shelley's Critical Prose*, ed. Bruce R. McElderry, Jr. (Lincoln: University of Nebraska Press, 1967), p. 16.

2. Three good examples are his poem "To Miss ——," cited in chap. 3, n. 25; his discourse in *The Task* VI.321ff.; and his amusing "The Poet, the Oyster, and Sensitive Plant."

3. *William Cowper* (New York: Twayne, 1970), p. 173.

4. Aaron J. Rosanoff, *Manual of Psychiatry and Mental Hygiene*, 7th ed., rev. (New York: J. Wiley, 1938), pp. 593–601.

5. To Joseph Hill, Nov. 14, 1779, in *The Correspondence of William Cowper*, ed. Thomas Wright (London: Hodder and Stoughton, 1904), I, 165–66.

6. To William Unwin, Sept. 26, 1781, *Correspondence*, I, 358.

7. "Written Extempore on the Sea-Shore," in *Poems on Several Occasions* (London, 1762), p. 38.

8. In Cowper, *Poetical Works*, ed. H. S. Milford, 4th ed., corrected by Norma Russell (London: Oxford University Press, 1971), p. 650.

9. Oct. 10, 1784, *Correspondence*, II, 252. Cowper also expresses pride in his originality in a letter written to Unwin on Nov. 24, 1781: "Imitation, even of the best models, is my aversion" (ibid., I, 386). In two essays, Pierre Danchin emphasizes "full personal expression" as a motive for Cowper's poetry: "William Cowper's Poetic Purpose as Seen in His Letters," *English Studies*, 46 (1965), 235–44; and "Poetry as Speech: Some Reflections on the Poetic Style of William Cowper and William Wordsworth," in *Le Romantisme anglo-américain: Mélanges offerts à Louis Bonnerot*, ed. Roger Asselineau (Paris: Didier, 1971), pp. 69–84.

10. *Table Talk*, ll. 712–13, and *The Progress of Error*, ll. 11–12. All quotations from Cowper's poetry are from *Poetical Works*, ed. H. S. Milford, cited in n. 8.

11. Henry Mackenzie, *The Lounger* (June 18, 1785), in *The Works of Henry Mackenzie, Esq.* (Edinburgh, 1808), V, 186–87.

12. This is one form of what Morris Golden has called the "religious paradox" in Cowper's thought—the idea that true liberation, in life or in art, is produced by religiously inspired limitations; see Golden's excellent *In Search of Stability: The Poetry of William Cowper* (New York: Bookman, 1960), esp. pp. 78–118.

13. May 3, 1780, *Correspondence*, I, 185.

14. Patricia Meyer Spacks has provided extensive discussions of Cowper's religious interpretation of his experience and the combination of direct perception and moral symbolism in his imagery: see *The Poetry of Vision: Five Eighteenth-Century Poets* (Cambridge, Mass.: Harvard University Press, 1967), pp. 165–206, on Cowper's verse; and *Imagining a Self: Autobiography and Novel in Eighteenth-Century England* (Cambridge, Mass.: Harvard University Press, 1976), pp. 17, 28–56, 78, on his autobiography. Spacks's account of Cowper's method of shaping his experience

and giving it meaning is similar to my own, although she adopts a more favorable attitude toward it than do I.

15. Maurice J. Quinlan, *William Cowper: A Critical Life* (Minneapolis: University of Minnesota Press, 1953), p. 211, suggests of the sixth book of Cowper's *Task* that "here, and perhaps only here in all his verse, nature is regarded as a book of revelation wherein one may find indisputable evidence of God's existence and beneficence." But although Cowper seldom regards nature as real "revelation," he frequently relies on it as objective "evidence" without bothering to insist that only people inspired by grace can derive wisdom from it. He is free to rely as strongly as he does on natural imagery because he is at all times prepared to reconcile it with biblical teaching; as he says about *The Task* to his spiritual advisor Newton: "I have admitted into my description no images but what are scriptural" (Nov. 27, 1784, *Correspondence*, II, 272).

16. *William Cowper*, p. 138. Although I cannot agree with some of Free's conclusions about what he calls "the fusion of subjective and objective in *The Task*," he offers an interesting discussion of the poem's structure and imagery (pp. 100–42) and recognizes both Cowper's "practice of sublimating response to landscape in conventional moral and religious thought" (p. 121) and his tendency "to internalize conventional imagery and to use it as an extension of his own spiritual condition" (p. 187).

17. The famous "stricken deer" image appears in *The Task* III.108–20. In "The Stricken Deer and the Emblem Tradition," *Bulletin of the New York Public Library*, 75 (1971), 66–78, J. H. Owen argues that Cowper's use of this conventional emblem proceeded not from "imagistic spontaneity" but from a desire "to express commonly held values in a stabilizing form of art" and also to confer moral authority on his perceptions. Cowper's "spiritual dilemma directed him to search in normative patterns of expression for some saving core of belief." Owen suggests that the poet believed in a kind of emblematic "revealed morality in the natural world."

18. Quinlan provides an extensive review of Cowper's "compulsive" images in *William Cowper*, pp. 190–207, and "Cowper's Imagery," *Journal of English and Germanic Philology*, 47 (1948), 276–85. Quinlan asserts, quite correctly, that the imagery with which Cowper expresses his observations does not necessarily reflect "the inherent characteristics" of what he views (*William Cowper*, p. 229), and he stresses the "highly subjective" nature of Cowper's use of biblical images ("Cowper's Imagery," p. 285).

19. Jan. 13, 1784, *Correspondence*, II, 146–47.

20. See the poems "On the Receipt of My Mother's Picture out of Norfolk," ll. 100–05, and "Yardley Oak," ll. 144–51; and Cowper's letter to Lady Hesketh, Aug. 27, 1795, *Correspondence*, IV, 489–90.

21. See the following Olney Hymns: "Welcome Cross," "Temptation," "Welcome to the Table," and "My Soul Thirsteth for God." For Cowper's use, both before and after the Olney Hymns, of images of being lost at sea, consult Quinlan, *William Cowper*, pp. 194–99, 231–32; and Charles Ryskamp, *William Cowper of the Inner*

Temple, Esq.: A Study of His Life and Works to the Year 1768 (Cambridge: Cambridge University Press, 1959), pp. 106–08.

22. *In Search of Stability,* pp. 164, 168. Golden's book offers an interesting account of Cowper's mental preoccupations as projected in his images of the outside world.

23. *Diary, Reminiscences, and Correspondence,* ed. Thomas Sadler, 3rd ed. (London, 1872), I, 339.

24. To Lady Hesketh, May 15, 1786, *Correspondence,* III, 35.

25. *The Life and Letters of William Cowper, Esq.* (London, 1835), pp. 429, 4. The anonymous writer of the preface to an edition of the *Memoir of the Early Life of William Cowper, Esq.* (London: R. Edwards, 1816) also asserts that Cowper's difficulties originated in an "excessive sensibility" (p. vii).

26. "On Thomson and Cowper," *Lectures on the English Poets,* in *The Complete Works of William Hazlitt,* ed. P. P. Howe, V (1930; rpt., New York: AMS Press, 1967), 95.

27. William Free's comment is apposite: "In Cowper, feeling springs not from a general benevolence toward mankind or from social impulses but from a deep sense of personal involvement. He experiences intense emotion because he cannot separate himself from the predicament of the drowning sailor" (*William Cowper,* p. 170).

Chapter 8
Self as Creative Genius: William Blake

1. Annotations to Berkeley's *Siris,* in *The Poetry and Prose of William Blake,* ed. David V. Erdman (Garden City, N.Y.: Doubleday, 1970), p. 653; and in *Complete Writings,* ed. Geoffrey Keynes (London: Oxford University Press, 1971), p. 774. All quotations are from the Erdman edition. Page numbers for each edition are cited parenthetically in the text as E and K respectively, preceded, in references to the works in illuminated printing, by plate number and, for poetry, by line number within each plate. References to *There Is No Natural Religion* and *All Religions Are One,* however, cite plate numbers according to the arrangement of G. E. Bentley, Jr., *Blake Books* (Oxford: Clarendon Press, 1977), pp. 79–86, 441–47.

2. "Blake and the Senses," *Studies in Romanticism,* 5 (1965), 12.

3. It is important to define such words as "mysticism" carefully. By this term I do not mean a belief in supernatural powers or influences, but a belief in mental powers that are not limited by natural laws as they are commonly understood. Any generalization about Blake is questionable, but I have attempted to base my conclusions on a study of the whole body of his writings while making due allowance for development of ideas and changes of emphasis from one work to another. I do think, however, that for the most part his later works show an expansion rather than a reversal of the basic ideas in his earlier works.

4. "Blake's Tree of Knowledge Grows Out of the Enlightenment," *Enlightenment Essays,* 3 (1972), 71–84. Blake's critics have often discussed this general topic. Nor-

throp Frye, for instance, in *Fearful Symmetry: A Study of William Blake* (Princeton: Princeton University Press, 1947), characterizes "the primacy [Locke] gives to sense experience" as a "Blakean" quality (p. 187) and considers the similarities between Berkeley's ideas and Blake's (pp. 14–15, 30). Bernard Blackstone, *English Blake* (Cambridge: Cambridge University Press, 1949), discusses Berkeley at length and finds "pure Blake doctrine" and the probable "source of many of Blake's ideas" in *The Principles of Human Knowledge;* yet he regards Berkeley as "a born Platonist" (pp. 334n, 336). Peter F. Fisher finds Blake's epistemology similar in some respects to that of the empiricists, and he distinguishes it from Platonism — *The Valley of Vision: Blake as Prophet and Revolutionary* (Toronto: University of Toronto Press, 1961), pp. 49–50. John H. Sutherland, in "Blake's 'Mental Traveller,'" *ELH*, 22 (1955), 137, considers Blake's system similar to Berkeley's in its supposition that "the only reality is psychological reality." Kathleen Raine, who views Blake primarily within the context of the "Perennial Philosophy," finds many connections between Blake and Berkeley; see *Blake and Tradition* (Princeton: Princeton University Press, 1968), esp. II, 106–50; and *Berkeley, Blake and the New Age* (Ipswich: Golgonooza Press, 1977). Yet she emphasizes the idea that Berkeley "is rooted in the Neoplatonic and Hermetic tradition to which Blake also turned" (*Blake and Tradition,* II, 102). Leonard Trawick, "Blake's Empirical Occult," *The Wordsworth Circle,* 8 (1977), 161–71, itemizes Blake's similarities to other thinkers and concludes that although "Blake does have many affinities with the occult traditions, his own view of reality is ultimately inimical to them. His ontology is radically empirical in the same sense that Berkeley's is" (p. 162).

5. *Energy and the Imagination: A Study of the Development of Blake's Thought* (Oxford: Clarendon Press, 1970), pp. 26–27.

6. Themistius' argument is that because "the forms are the beings" and "it is the soul that imparteth forms to matter," then "all beings are in the soul" — *The Works of George Berkeley, Bishop of Cloyne,* ed. A. A. Luce and T. E. Jessop, V (London: Nelson, 1953), 143. Blake adopts this doctrine of "forms" only with the proviso that "Forms must be apprehended by Sense or the Eye of Imagination."

7. Keynes, ed., *Complete Writings,* p. 923; Blackstone, *English Blake,* p. 337n.

8. *Blake's Night: William Blake and the Idea of Pastoral* (Cambridge, Mass.: Belknap-Harvard University Press, 1973), p. 287.

9. The word "individualist" carries many different connotations, and I think it is important to emphasize the fact that I am here evaluating Blake's "individualist" psychology and not his "individualist" ethical and political beliefs, which may be evaluated on other grounds.

10. Blake's use of the word "true" is susceptible of various interpretations. He obviously means that the Poetic Genius is the "best" or "most proper" self; but he also means that it is the "fundamental" self, which, as he says, gives man his "form." J. Middleton Murry notices this issue in his consideration of some of the problems that Blake raises by viewing the Poetic Genius as a principle of individuation — *William Blake* (London: Cape, 1933), pp. 25–29.

11. The idea of the tractate's indebtedness to Lavater has recently received powerful support from Richard J. Schroyer, "The 1788 Publication Date of Lavater's *Aphorisms on Man,*" *Blake*, 11 (1977), 23–26.

12. Cf. Blake's comment on the renewal of the essence of "identical" characters in different ages: "Accident ever varies, Substance can never suffer change nor decay" (*A Descriptive Catalogue;* E 523, K 567).

13. On characters as states, see Martin Price, *To the Palace of Wisdom: Studies in Order and Energy from Dryden to Blake* (Garden City, N.Y.: Doubleday, 1964), pp. 406, 410, 424.

14. Lowery, *Windows of the Morning: A Critical Study of William Blake's "Poetical Sketches," 1783* (New Haven: Yale University Press, 1940), p. 122; Schorer, *William Blake: The Politics of Vision* (New York: Henry Holt, 1946), p. 424.

15. *William Blake* (1961; rpt., Hamden, Conn.: Archon Books, 1967), p. 118.

16. *Fearful Symmetry*, p. 23. Fisher makes a similar comment in *The Valley of Vision*, p. 107. Although Schorer states that Blake "revived the old theory of innate ideas," he distinguishes Blake's belief in innate "capacities" from a belief in innate "concepts" — *Politics of Vision*, p. 445.

17. Paley, *Energy and the Imagination*, p. 226, makes a similar connection between Blake and Shaftesbury, although his views on innate ideas appear to differ from my own. See also Price, *To the Palace of Wisdom*, pp. 80, 419–21, on the nature of the "true self" in Shaftesbury and Blake.

18. Schorer, *Politics of Vision*, p. 347, also remarks "the grave failure of objectivity," proceeding from an undue faith in personal inspiration, that allowed Blake "to superimpose the Hayley quarrel" on *Milton*. Schorer's work, the most extensive account of Blake's individualism, criticizes at length the poetic difficulties attributable to Blake's reliance on personal vision and spontaneous impulse; see esp. pp. 395–460.

19. Blake to Thomas Butts, Apr. 25, 1803 (E 697, K 823). In *Jerusalem*, Blake writes: "We who dwell on Earth can do nothing of ourselves, every thing is conducted by Spirits, no less than Digestion or Sleep" (3; E 144, K 621).

20. Ronald L. Grimes has aptly said of Blake's final narrative method that "the causal and developmental linkage that one might expect of epic is simply not there. The 'wherefores' do not tell 'why,' and the 'thens' seem only to mean 'and'" — "Time and Space in Blake's Major Prophecies," in *Blake's Sublime Allegory: Essays on The Four Zoas, Milton, Jerusalem*, ed. Stuart Curran and Joseph Anthony Wittreich, Jr. (Madison: University of Wisconsin Press, 1973), p. 64. As Grimes suggests, however, Blake's belief in activity "conducted by Spirits" (or the Spirit) allows him to emphasize the possibility of an almost miraculously "uncaused," spontaneous redemption (pp. 59–81).

21. "The Formal Art of *The Four Zoas*," in *Blake's Visionary Forms Dramatic*, ed. David V. Erdman and John E. Grant (Princeton: Princeton University Press, 1970), p. 373.

22. The distinction between sincere, properly directed sympathy and passive or

hypocritical pity is commonly, and correctly, observed by Blake's critics. The most extensive discussions of his view of sympathy are provided by D. G. Gillham in *Blake's Contrary States: The "Songs of Innocence and of Experience" as Dramatic Poems* (Cambridge: Cambridge University Press, 1966) and *William Blake* (Cambridge: Cambridge University Press, 1973), esp. pp. 61–91. Gillham properly contrasts spontaneous giving of emotion with self-centered projection of one's own feelings. In distinguishing Blake's concept of sympathy from that of his eighteenth-century predecessors, however, Gillham overemphasizes the "rationalistic" quality of the eighteenth-century concept and unduly mysticizes the type of sympathy found in Blake's *Songs of Innocence.*

23. *Blake's Apocalypse: A Study in Poetic Argument* (Garden City, N.Y.: Doubleday, 1963), p. 170.

24. In an essay on mirror imagery in *Urizen*, Robert E. Simmons emphasizes the problem, which I have discussed in connection with Cowper's poetry, of an infinite regress of subject-object reflections — "*Urizen:* The Symmetry of Fear," in *Visionary Forms Dramatic*, pp. 146–73. Hazard Adams, writing on "The Crystal Cabinet" and "The Golden Net," also discusses this problem — *William Blake: A Reading of the Shorter Poems* (Seattle: University of Washington Press, 1963), pp. 121–31. Simmons is not concerned with the issue of sympathy, but Adams considers the Blakean distinction between a debasing "pity" and creative action.

25. *The Mirror*, Nos. 99 and 100, in *The Works of Henry Mackenzie, Esq.* (Edinburgh, 1808), IV, 391–92, 378.

26. John Beer, *Blake's Visionary Universe* (Manchester: Manchester University Press, 1969), pp. 81–82, describes Urizen's laws as eighteenth-century benevolence destroying itself.

27. I am obviously in agreement with Harold Bloom, *Blake's Apocalypse*, p. 293, that the Host is "a Urizenic figure" offering "cannibal fare." Sutherland, "Blake's 'Mental Traveller,'" pp. 141–42, sees the Host, in this passage, as primarily a tyrant delighted in others' pain — a conception that, in Blake's terms, is not entirely inconsistent with my idea of the Host as a man of Urizenic sensibility.

28. Ben Jones, "Blake on Gray: Outlines of Recognition," in *Fearful Joy: Papers from the Thomas Gray Bicentenary Conference at Carleton University*, ed. James Downey and Ben Jones (Montreal: McGill-Queen's University Press, 1974), pp. 127–35, provides an interesting discussion of Blake's disapproval of Gray's attitude toward human limitations.

29. On Blake's Albion versus Hobbes's Leviathan, see Paley, *Energy and the Imagination*, pp. 197–99.

30. John Howard, *Blake's "Milton": A Study in the Selfhood* (Rutherford, N.J.: Fairleigh Dickinson University Press, 1976), pp. 176–78, notices the similarity between Blake's terminology and Hartley's, and proposes additional reasons for distinguishing Hartley's concept of "self-annihilation" from Blake's. He also recognizes the paradoxical quality of Hartleian "self-annihilation." It may be questioned, however, whether Blake's conflation of self-annihilation and self-assertion is not more

paradoxical than Hartley's; whether, in some sense, Blakean "selflessness" is not something different from the "antithesis of self-interest" that Howard considers it.

31. On "projection" and "disguise" in the Nurse's reactions, cf. Price, *To the Palace of Wisdom,* p. 397; and E. D. Hirsch, Jr., *Innocence and Experience: An Introduction to Blake* (New Haven: Yale University Press, 1964), pp. 232–33.

32. *William Blake: His Philosophy and Symbols* (1924; rpt., Gloucester, Mass.: Peter Smith, 1958), p. 307; *A Blake Dictionary: The Ideas and Symbols of William Blake* (New York: Dutton, 1971), p. 174. Ben Jones, discussing Blake's attempt to escape from "sensibility," considered as an awareness of life's evanescence, suggests that Gray's Stoke Poges may have its "counterpart in the pastoral Vales of Har to which Thel returns to continue brooding on her extinction" — "Blake on Gray: Outlines of Recognition," in *Fearful Joy,* p. 134n.

33. In an interesting essay on the *Tiriel* illustrations, Robert N. Essick characterizes Har and Heva as representatives of a melancholy sensibility and draws attention to their face-to-face position in two of the designs as a symbol of "limited perspective" and "total self-involvement." "Sympathetic involvement" might, however, more accurately express what Blake is apparently satirizing. Although Essick does not consider the relevance of the eighteenth-century ideal of sympathy, and the art based upon it, to the *Tiriel* designs, he observes that "Har and Heva have contracted their vision to a transfixed gaze at each other or at their own reflection." See "The Altering Eye: Blake's Vision in the *Tiriel* Designs," in *William Blake: Essays in Honour of Sir Geoffrey Keynes,* ed. Morton D. Paley and Michael Phillips (Oxford: Clarendon Press, 1973), pp. 50–65.

34. "To Miss ——," ll. 45–48, 66–68, in *Poetical Works,* ed. H. S. Milford, 4th ed., corrected by Norma Russell (London: Oxford University Press, 1971), pp. 286, 287.

35. A critic who has traced literary problems of the self from the eighteenth to the twentieth century speaks of "the secular working religion of modern self-conscious people — a religion that recognizes the spiritual problem of our time as a problem of identity and that seems always . . . to regard salvation as self-realization" — Robert Langbaum, *The Mysteries of Identity: A Theme in Modern Literature* (New York: Oxford University Press, 1977), p. 353.

Index

Adams, Hazard, 179n24
Addison, Joseph, 14
Árdal, Páll S., 28
Aristotle, 110

Bate, Walter Jackson, 41
Bateson, F. W., 170n25
Beattie, James, 20–24, 51, 85
Beer, John, 179n26
Berkeley, George, 10, 15, 16, 21, 128–29, 131–32, 138
Blackstone, Bernard, 129, 177n4
Blair, Hugh, 52, 53–54, 105, 164nn21, 22, 165n37
Blake, William: on conscience, 23, 141; and the sublime, 120, 136–37; relation to eighteenth-century psychology, 127–32, 134, 137–38, 143–53; principal discussion of, 127–56; mentioned, 10, 12, 45–46, 47, 57–58
—Works: *All Religions Are One*, 130–31, 133–34; Annotations to Berkeley, 127, 129; to Lavater, 133–34, 138–39, 143; to Reynolds, 24, 133, 137–38; to Swedenborg, 127–28, 132, 134; to Watson, 141; to Wordsworth, 112, 143; Correspondence, 139–40, 141; "Crystal Cabinet, The," 179n24; *Descriptive Catalogue, A*, 178n12; *Europe*, 144, 149; *Four Zoas, The*, 45, 142, 143–44; "Golden Net, The," 179n24; *Jerusalem*, 129, 132, 135,

Blake, William (*cont.*)
136, 137, 142, 144, 149–50, 151, 178n19; *Marriage of Heaven and Hell, The*, 128, 132, 143, 146–47, 155; "Mental Traveller, The," 142–43, 147–48, 151; *Milton*, 129, 150–51, 178n18; *On Homer's Poetry*, 146; *Song of Los, The*, 152; *Songs of Experience*, 144, 151–52; *Songs of Innocence*, 57, 144, 146; *Thel, The Book of*, 141, 180n32; *There Is No Natural Religion*, 7, 130–31, 132; *Tiriel*, 152–55; *Urizen, The Book of*, 139, 144–46, 147, 153; *Vision of the Last Judgment, A*, 129, 134–36; *Visions of the Daughters of Albion*, 141, 148
Bloom, Harold, 145, 179n27
Bogel, Fredric V., 37
Bolingbroke, Henry St. John, 1st viscount, 85–87, 92
Bonstetten, Charles-Victor, 88
Borges, Jorge Luis, 156
Brady, Frank, 171n31
Braudy, Leo, 167n3, 169n24
Bredvold, Louis I., 166n46
Brissenden, R. F., 22, 54, 64, 159n7, 163n53, 167n6
Bronson, Bertrand H., 172n2
Buddhism, 3–4
Burke, Edmund, 29, 101
Butler, Joseph, 22

181